Love, Laughter and Tears

Betty O'Neill

Betty O'Neill 09/03/2024.

Love, Laughter and Tears

Betty O'Neill

British Library Cataloguing in Publication Data.
A catalogue record for this book is available from the British Library

ISBN 978 0 86071 927 4

Editing: Chris and Trish Gannon

Cover design: Betty O'Neill

Printed in the UK

I dedicate this book to my husband, Michael,

without whose encouragement and

patience my words would have remained

unspoken and my stories untold.

Contents

The Artist

Betty O'Neill grew up on Station Road, Ilkeston, the eldest daughter of Gordon and Doris Holmes.

She was educated at the Chaucer Infants and Junior School, and later Hallcroft Technical School.

Betty studied art at the Bath Academy of Art, and when she qualified, she taught art in Ilkeston and Nottingham Schools, until she took early retirement through ill health.

Her exhibited work is part of work created of her memories of growing up in a town much changed by half a century or so. The work has been painstakingly created over several years by Betty whilst recovering from a serious illness which changed her life forever.

The work was never really intended for public display. However, the Stroke Association entered it into the Susie Halks Memorial Award for Art, where she garnered second place, awarded by the Duke of Kent. She also received an award for inspirational art.

These pictures were originally created for her family and are something of a history lesson on how we used to live and how things have changed so dramatically in a relatively short time.

Betty painted the pictures in a light-hearted way from memory, as she would have done when she was a young girl.

If you remember things slightly differently, you may well be right - our memories can trip us up, and become, perhaps, a little rose-tinted with the passage of time.

There are no great works of art in this exhibition, nor were there meant to be, just her memories of a very happy childhood. Betty hopes you enjoy looking at the pictures and that they might bring back happy memories for those who were around then.

National award for stroke victim's inspirational art

Retired teacher who taught herself to paint again is 'over the moon'

BATH SPA UNIVERSITY

Betty O'Neill

has been awarded the Honorary Degree of

Bachelor of Arts in Education

by

Bath Spa University

in recognition of outstanding services within the Education sector

1 March 2022

Vice-Chancellor   University Secretary

Acknowledgement

I would like to pay tribute to my wife, Betty, whose dogged determination to uncomplainingly accept whatever life's misfortunes have thrown at her, and to still keep smiling, is unbelievable. The title of her book, though, should be 'Blood, Sweat and Tears' - her stories have literally taken years to get out of her and written down.

A brave woman.

Michael O'Neill

Foreword

It is both an honour and a privilege to make this small contribution to this remarkable book by Betty O'Neill. Betty was born in Ilkeston, a small town on the Derbyshire and Nottinghamshire border. In those days the men worked mostly in the coal mines or the steel works and the associated industries. Many of the women were employed in the Hosiery factories. Throughout it was hard work with long hours. Most of the domestic housing relied on outside lavatories and a tin bath that was often put to use by the coal fire in the kitchen. This was long before the advent of home telephones, fridges, television or many other conveniences now taken for granted.

Life was tough but relationships that were established early in life endured through childhood, education, military service, employment and old age. Good things were shared and celebrated and in challenging times support and care was given. Everyone knew the name of the shopkeeper, the bus driver and conductor and the staff at the railway station. The community held together.

Betty trained as a teacher and taught art in the local schools. When later in life her illness restricted her speech she set about producing for her family a text beautifully illustrated by her distinctive paintings. The reality is that by her skill and tenacity she has produced a great deal more. Her book is a remarkable record of the social history of our country principally during the 1940s and 1950s. The combination of text and paintings makes the book both informative and attractive. It illustrates well the journey large parts of our country has travelled during the lifetime of Betty and Michael. The paintings are a special pleasure. I commend it most warmly.

The Rt. Hon. The Lord Laming CBE PC DL

Welcome

These pictures were originally created for my children, grandchildren and, hopefully, further descendants. I wanted them to have some idea of how we used to live and how things have changed dramatically in a relatively short time. The description is a history lesson, if you like, for people who were not even born and have no real idea of how we lived. I have tried to create these pictures from memory and painted them in a light-hearted way. Just the way I would have done when I was a young girl.

Is that you or your granny blowing into the winter warmer in the winter of '47 picture? Or perhaps it's you having a donkey ride in Chaucer school playground. What has that girl dropped at the dinner table? Do some of the girls not have water glasses on the table? I wonder why? Is that your dad in the market, taking his library books back to the library?

Perhaps you knew the woman who has just bought a wreath. You can't see her? What about the woman in the fur coat? That's something you don't see nowadays!

If you can't see all these things going on, you are not really looking. Go on, have another look.

Was that you fooling around in the cabins at the swimming baths?

Or, perhaps, that is your gran having to go to the lav just as she's sat down at the anniversary.

Was that your mam or gran coming in the chapel door, pregnant, with your brother or sister? Wasn't the organist good?

My dad and Dinky, our dog, were always watching from outside, whatever the weather. Did you have a peg rug like the one in our living room? Can't see most of these things? Oh dear, never mind.

If you were in a picture, or remember them just like that, I am glad you have enjoyed them and the memories they have brought back.

CHAPTER 1

Our House

Where my stories and pictures began

My house was on Station Road on the corner of Blake Street, Ilkeston, a row of eight semi-detached, three-story houses. These eight houses were quite a lot bigger than many of the terraced houses in the streets around us.

One end was Barnes the butchers, now a sweet shop for many years and the other end of the row was our house, which was directly opposite the Co-op store, which was very handy for Mam collecting the rations.

I lived in the house with my mam and dad, grandmother (Mama), my younger sister, Cynthia, and my three uncles who were my mam's brothers and my mama's sons (who had returned from the war), and our little dog, Dinky.

My Home, Station Road. Circa 1948

Our house was always warm and happy, and there was always a lot of noise and laughter and sometimes angry rows that never lasted long but made me very anxious whenever they did occur. Dad was always up early to go on early shift at the Cossall pit.

We had a little garden at the front, a small back yard, a coalhouse and an outside lavatory, or lav as we used to say, and no bathroom. We had a front door on the side of the house, which was never used, and two steps down from our back yard onto Blake Street, which ran directly down to Johnny's (Wash Meadow) where there were allotments that ran the whole length of the meadow down to the canal where Millership Way now runs.

The allotments are long gone; I don't know why they didn't survive since the land wasn't taken for some other use when other allotments around the town were highly prized. The streets around us seemed to constantly have the lovely smell of bonfires, especially in the autumn if the wind was blowing our way and the gardeners were clearing up after a busy summer.

Mr Pritchet lived on Canal Street and worked his allotment, which was situated on the other side of the canal and Station Road, on the Ropewalk alongside the others there. He sold much of his produce and was renowned for the quality of his vegetables, mainly because of his friendship with Mr Smith who kept his pigs alongside his allotment and was always barrowing pig muck from Mr Smith's sty and spreading it over his beds. He could often be seen and heard around Ilkeston and over to Cotmanhay, pushing his barrow filled with vegetables that he had grown on his allotment, often returning to fill his barrow again, so popular was his produce. His celery, which Mrs Pritchit used to scrub and clean in the basement of their house on Canal Street until it was clean and white, was much sought-after as it was all ready for the table.

He had regular customers usually doing his round on Saturday and Sundays and could be heard shouting, 'celery, celery, get your celery here!' On quiet Sundays, his loud voice could be heard streets away and housewives would nip out or send a child to get something. He always came home with an empty barrow from his trips. This was the period after the war when people were still encouraged to grow vegetables to help our food supplies. He must have walked miles, and he was an elderly man, but money was very tight for many, and as the saying goes, 'Needs must when the devil drives.'

On the other side of where Wash Meadow allotments were is the road now named Millership Way. Back then the spur line, which ran from the mainline at the Ilkeston Junction to Ilkeston Town Station, was at the bottom of Bath Street. The entrance was somewhere alongside where the public toilets used to be. You could catch the train at the junction to ride up to the town station for a couple of coppers. Lads, who had been train spotting at the junction, would often do if they had a few pennies to spare.

I could never see the point in writing down train numbers or keeping little reference books to look up the passing train.

I didn't know any girls who did that, it was a boy thing. Further up the line to the crossing near Potters Lock, you would sometimes see young kids waiting patiently by the side of the line for the next train to come. It would thunder past to flatten the pennies that they had placed on the line, making them twice the original size. They would whoop with glee when the train had passed as they recovered their enormous pennies. Adults passing by didn't bat an eye, health and safety was unheard of and common sense was expected to prevail, with the older ones looking after the young ones. Strangely enough it seemed to work, most of the time, even if some of the things they got up to would now be deemed to be highly dangerous.

I never did this. Any spare money I had would be saved to fund my obsession, the 'Pictures'. If I could have gone every evening of the week, and to the 'tanner rush' on Saturdays, I would have been in heaven.

On the other side of the spur line was the gasometer that rose and fell with the amount of gas in it. Dad would say, when just the skeleton of the gasometer stood with the balloon sunk low, 'Ey up! Pressure's down today.' The gas works on the other side of Belfield Street made the gas and it was stored in the gasometer to supply the whole of Ilkeston.

A high wall used to encircle the gasworks, and kids who lived nearby would sometimes scrawl their initials with a sucker stick or something on the wall with the tar that was melting on the road on a hot summer's day. I think there must have been many adults walking down Rutland Street, passing that old gasworks wall before it was knocked down, smiling to themselves and remembering, when they saw their initials, still there on the wall in black tar that they had laboriously scrawled on some hot summer day as children, so long ago. I know I did.

Happy days.

CHAPTER 2

After The War

My mam's brothers, and Mama's sons served in the forces during the war; two served together in the Army and one in the Navy.

My dad's brother, Ken, also served in the Navy. He was awarded the Legion d'Honneur by the French government for his part in D -Day and we were all very proud and pleased for him. He wanted no fuss though and it arrived by post and was quietly put away with his other medals.

My uncle, Bill Osborne or 'Boss', as his brothers called him because he was the eldest, served with his brother, Ted, in the Army and as 'regulars' they fought across North Africa and Europe. Boss rose to the rank of sergeant major by the end of the war. They tried to look out for each other as best they could in the circumstances. Mama was constantly worrying about them all whilst they were away. It wasn't just a few months they were away either, it was years.

I had my very first letter from my Uncle Ted, the younger brother in the Army and I still have it to this day. I would lie in the bed I had shared with

Mama from when I was born, and she would read it to me again and again. He said that he was lying in a foxhole in the desert writing the letter, with his mate, 'Jock', who was getting them something to eat. He told me to be a good girl and look after my baby sister. I never tired of having it read to me. After the war ended and they eventually came home on leave, they sent strict instructions that the practice of decorating the house with flags and banners to welcome them home was not to be followed or they wouldn't even come in.

But they did celebrate, big time. They were up town, going from pub to pub meeting old friends and comrades. Once, arriving back more than a little inebriated, they carried Mama's beautiful wind-up gramophone from the front room, ignoring everyone shouting, "be careful don't scratch it!" I can vividly remember them both singing Jerusalem with their lovely tenor voices, along with the Great Caruso on Mama's old 78 vinyl record. It was a very early version of karaoke, I suppose!

Poor old Dad, who had to be away to the pit early next morning, looked very fed-up throughout their antics, wishing they would all go to bed. However, when they loudly started singing 'Keep the Red Flag Flying', Mama started to panic. 'Oh, stop it, our sons! If the police hear you they will think we are all communists.'

All too soon their leave ended, and they had to return, even after being away for so long. Thousands of young men who had signed up for the duration of the war were being demobbed so, being regulars, they had to wait a while before getting out of the army.

When they all came home for good, we all lived together, and it was great. Many children who were born while their fathers were away during the war found it difficult to accept this man who had suddenly appeared, imposing discipline on them – some of whom were unruly children, more used to a lax regime with their mam. We were lucky enough to have no such problem and, in fact, we were positively spoiled.

It was a sad day when, soon enough, they were getting married and leaving our house. Uncle Boss married and became the caretaker at Cotmanhay Infants and Junior School but sadly died at a young age. He had one son who later emigrated to Australia.

My uncle, Ted Osborne, eventually opened a hardware shop on Cotmanhay Road opposite Richmond Avenue. It's called Linda's Mini Market now. I think half of Ilkeston knew my Uncle Ted! He was a great raconteur and always had a tale to tell. Anything he hadn't got in stock you could guarantee he would get for you. People would go into his shop to purchase something and by the time they had finished chatting and putting the world to rights, they had probably missed their bus, forgotten what they had gone in for and left with an item that they hadn't realised they wanted!

I think they must have based Ronnie Barker's 'Open All Hours' on Ted's shop. Ted would also deliver paraffin all over the Cotmanhay area. He married Freda and had two boys and a girl and lived in the house which was part of the shop. He died in 2001 and, like all of them, is sadly missed.

Ilkeston in the forties and fifties was awash with men like my uncles - men who had served together, sometimes in both world wars. Most are sadly no longer with us. They experienced things together that civilians couldn't ever really grasp.

But they wouldn't go on about war stories, and derring-do acts, usually only funny stories of things that had happened to them or someone they knew. Now more than ever in today's world such strength of character is needed, and we can all learn so much from their legacy.

CHAPTER 3

The Winters of 1947 and 1950

The winter of 1947 is often remembered as the one of the harshest winters in living memory. From 22nd January to 17th March, snow fell somewhere every day in the UK. German prisoners were kept at Wollaton Park and were used to clear minor roads and troops even tried using flamethrowers to clear the snow. Even Buckingham Palace was lit by candlelight due to power cuts and fuel shortages across the country.

The winter of 1950 was one of the snowiest winters of the last century. As children, we loved it. Hilly Holies off Cantelupe Road was the best place to go sledging, down the hill at high speed and across the road, crashing into the bank of snow at the railings. Long slides, practically the length of Blake Street on the icy pavement, would be made. Kids sliding down, their arms 'windmilling' to keep their balance, that is until some misery guts would come out with a dustpan full of hot ashes and put paid to the slide!

There were fuel shortages too (as the daughter of a coal miner - not at our house) and long queues formed on Rutland Street each Saturday morning as people waited for the Gasworks to open and start selling coke at sixpence a bag. People came from far afield, dragging sledges or pushing old barrows; anything that could be dragged or pushed was pressed into service. My husband remembers trudging from their new house on Cotmanhay estate, which they had moved into when his dad returned from the war, pushing a makeshift barrow his dad had made (badly!)

His mum had the bright idea of sewing two or three sack bags together to get a good six-penneth of coke. The two men filling the sacks at the coke delivery chute laughed and thought this was a good wheeze, and filled the sack to the brim, tying it with difficulty. It took three or four of them to lift and place the giant bag on top of the thing his dad had made and rather optimistically called a barrow!

His father was rather pleased with himself, even though they struggled to push the barrow through the snowy streets on the three-mile journey home. That is until the axle on his contrivance snapped about halfway home on Cotmanhay road. My husband recalls crying with the bitter cold and his dad, with a dewdrop of sweat on the end of his nose, standing looking with despair at the giant sack spilling out coke, half lying on the road.

Within half an hour or so three men had returned with a proper barrow, loaded the sack and helped push it (with child perched on top) up onto the estate and home.

Most of Ilkeston's residents travelled together on public transport commuting to their work at mines, ironworks and the hosiery factories. Many drank together too in Ilkeston's pubs, having probably served together in the war. Even perhaps if they didn't know each other then I think the spirit of camaraderie was still strong in that rather insular community of the time. The wartime slogan used to be 'we're all in it together'; I think in the late forties and fifties people thought they were still in it together, that's what they used to say at our house anyway.

It was around this time that the Korean War broke out. Most of the lads who had returned from the war were reservists. My father-in-law, a reservist too, was in a blind panic. Not at the thought of going back, but because he had come home from the war and got a job as a Barton's bus driver.

Rationing was still on and companies with staff who wore a uniform just couldn't source the material to have them made.

My father-in law, using his initiative, had his military uniform dyed brown - Barton's colours. He didn't think he was going to get a very good reception going back to the depot looking like a chocolate soldier. "My stripes would have been gone faster than you could say Jack Flash," he said. Luckily they were never called up and after driving through some of the harshest weather of 1950 he soldiered on to swelter through the summer in his dress uniform!

The Winter of '47

CHAPTER 4

A Fowl Tale

*My younger sister was small, very pretty and, I
think it is fair to say, spoiled by everyone.*

It was quite normal, when I was a child, for parents to send their offspring
out with the eldest child, who was tasked with the duty of keeping younger
siblings occupied and safe. I think we have all done things when we were
young that we later regretted and there are a few of us who did some things
that would remain with us for the rest of our lives; not allowed to forget
that one little misdeed.

And so, it was to be my poor judgment of circumstances, one morning, that
would come to haunt me for the rest of my life. Something my parents
(mother) would ceaselessly bring up in times of anger or stress. Today, only
that small, pretty and unwitting star of the show is left to remind me what I
did that morning (which, she still does.) I suppose it must have been a little
traumatic for her…

One sunny morning we were sent out with the usual words: 'look after your
sister!' followed by instructions to 'just nip and get this, that and the other.'
Never just one errand but several.

We met up on the street with my friend, Joan, who also had errands to run for her mam. 'We are going to be all morning dragging her round with us,' my friend sighed. We had planned to go over to the 'Ashes' or 'Potter's' at the bottom of Gordon Street to play on their tall swings and giant stone blocks which were strewn about.

'Can we go and see the chickens, our Bett?' my sister said. She was obsessed with Joan's mam's chickens, which were kept in a large pen at the bottom of Joan's garden. That was the moment that I had a brilliant brainwave. A moment in time that I am never to be rid of.

'Oh, what a good idea!' I said. My sister was always very happy to chat to the hens for ages.

'Would you like to go and sit in their little house and talk to them?' I said to her.

'Oh yes! Can I, our Bett?' her eyes sparkling with excitement.

'Of course, you can! In you go, sit in the corner and speak softly to them. Perhaps you could sing them a little song. We will be back in a little while. We're just nipping to do some errands, so you enjoy yourself.'

I locked the pen door behind her, and we left her, chattering happily to the hens. I suppose we might have got a little distracted doing our errands, catching up with friends we met along the way, enjoying the odd game of hopscotch or standing in a line of girls waiting to run under a skipping rope. The morning seemed to fly by.

'Do you think your Cynthia is okay?' Joan asked as we were finishing our errands. I cannot describe the shock those words had on me. I had completely forgotten about her. We had, without question, been more than the 'not long' we had promised. We raced back as fast as we could and to our horror, we found the pen empty. The hens were all huddled together in a corner clucking mournfully. I was paralysed. I didn't know what to do. Joan was also panicking - she had spied her mam storming down the garden path.

'You bad girls!' she shouted. 'You! Inside. Now!' She pointed at Joan, who did just that, exiting swiftly, stage left. Joan's mother moved on to me. 'You. Get home. Your mam is waiting for you. Just look at the state of our hens. We will never get eggs again by the looks of them. Your sister has been screaming her head off for ages. They're terrified. Not to mention everyone in the street wondering what was going on. It sounded as though she was being murdered. You're for it when you get home. Your mam is absolutely furious!'

I reluctantly sloped off home only to find my sister merrily playing in the back yard.

'You aren't half going to cop it, our Bett!' she said cheerfully as I shut the gate. 'Mam's going to kill you.' I opened the back door and went in, shaking like a leaf, as our Mam tore into me.

'YOU WICKED GIRL!' she screamed. Even Mama, who always protected me from any trouble, had her head bent, pounding dough in a bowl, averting her gaze as the scene played out. 'Oh, save the tears', Mam glowered at me, 'you're going to need some for when your dad gets in!'

My sister suddenly appeared, sobbing bitterly. 'It was awful, Mam!' she whimpered. If she'd have been on the stage, she would have received a standing ovation for that performance. Right on cue, in came Dad, who had already had the story regaled to him by the neighbours. He summed up the situation immediately.

'Oh, what's going on now?' he said. The whole sorry tale was given to him in detail.

'Oh, my duck!' he said, picking up my sister, 'did they peck you?'

'Oh yes, they did, Dad. I'm covered in peck marks!' (Forget the standing ovation, she was now going for an Oscar…) 'Ah, well! Now you know what it's like for me living in this house with all you women. Peck! Peck! Peck! All the time. Come on, Boris, that's enough now.' (Mam's name was Doris but Dad affectionately called her Boris.)

'She won't do that again, will you?' he said, giving my shoulder a squeeze. I relaxed, knowing then that I was off the hook.

'Is that it?' Mam said. 'You're as soft as cart grease with them!'

Mama looked up, relieved, and shook her head at me. Perhaps it was my imagination but I'm pretty sure my 'angelic' sister raised an eyebrow and cocked her head slightly to one side, as if to say, 'take that!'

At that time my sister or I had not heard the saying 'revenge is a dish best served cold.' I do believe, however, it was at that precise moment my sister realised revenge was sweet whichever way it was served. Seeing her sister getting it in the neck from all sides made her sibling satisfaction levels rocket off the scale. So, for one more time, and in print, on public record - sorry Cyn - I won't do it again.

CHAPTER 5

All in a Day's Play

Our street (and most streets come to that when school was out) were always full of children playing and often you would hear angry housewives coming out and shouting at the top of their voices for the kids to go away and play on someone else's front.

'My husband's on nights,' they would yell.

It was safe for the children playing out in the streets in those days. There were no cars parked and the streets were empty. Only the wealthy would own a car and no one wealthy lived around us, apart from Mr Smith, the shopkeeper, at the top of Blake Street. Mr Smith wasn't wealthy, but he was fairly well-off for the time. He once bought a brand-new car that he parked across the road from the shop, right outside our front door. Mam didn't mind. She used to stick her nose in the air when she went across to the Co-op; she imagined that people thought it was ours! One-upmanship was rife at the time when none of the families had much. The eleven-plus exams were a prime example of that.

We had an idyllic childhood, although money was always tight for Mam and Dad. We were always dressed well and fed well, never hit or smacked like many children of that era, although Mam could give you a good whipping with her tongue. Mama was the mother of everyone, and I loved her dearly. I had slept with her from birth, and she was, I thought, the mainstay of our family and my protector.

Mam had one fault that stayed with her and spoiled her life. She had a massive inferiority complex, and it was completely unfounded. She was a good mother and a hard-working woman, but she imagined everyone was better-off than she was. She thought she was too fat, (not true) and that people were looking down on her (also not true.) She had been an intelligent, young woman and had the opportunity to go to the grammar school, but the family couldn't afford it, and it was this, I think, that she always resented. So, Mam took any opportunity to show people she was as good as them and demonstrated this at my expense. When our year took the eleven-plus examination, her remark was: 'You had better pass, madam, I'm telling you.' Fortunately, I did, but with unimaginable consequences for me…

When I came home with the slip saying I had passed the exam, my uniform was bought the very next day. I was immediately placed in it: white blouse, navy skirt, white socks, my blazer with sleeves down to my fingertips ('you'll grow into it'), complete with beret and tie. I was then pushed out of the house and walked (paraded) up and down all our adjoining streets.

Mam's head was held high, and her chest pushed out, glowing with pride. I had held a handkerchief over my mouth and lowered my head in misery and shame. The sleeve of my arm was firmly grasped by Mam, ensuring no escape. All the kids were out playing, some sneering (especially those who hadn't passed) and they were 'gawking' at us. Curtains twitched as kids ran in to say, 'Quick, Mam! Look out the window!' It was unusual for a kid to be marched through the streets by an adult unless it was for some wrongdoing and parents were soon made aware of anything unusual that was happening on the street by their offspring.

As soon as we arrived home, Mam started for a second circuit, but I yanked myself free and ran into the house with Mam at my heels, ordering, 'Get that uniform off and put it on a hanger!' I went to my bedroom and had a good weep for the rest of the evening, completely mortified. Mam was as proud as punch and just couldn't understand her daughter's anguish.

My only saving grace was that word must have got round and two more girls were marched round the same circuit in full uniform in the days following, knocking me off the day's gossip.

Some mothers couldn't wait to get to the corner shop in the days following the eleven-plus results. This happened all over the country, from what I've heard, not just our neighbourhood, often finding they were running out of things three or four times a day as an excuse to get over there when another victim appeared! The refrain would go something like this: 'Oh how did Joey get on with his eleven-plus?' (knowing jolly well how every child in the school who had taken the exam had fared, her own having been quizzed extensively.) 'Oh, never mind, he would only have been miserable if he wasn't clever enough to be there!' before saying, nonchalantly. 'Oh yes mine passed - though she is quite clever.'

Mr Smith parked his car in front of our house to stop all the kids playing at the top of the street, nobody dared run around it or kick a ball near it. This had the planned effect of pushing all the kids further down the street in front of neighbours' houses lower down. It gave our end a bit of peace and quiet. If you've heard playtime at any primary school, you will have an idea of how noisy the streets would be when all the kids were home from school.

It was quite normal to see boys having a football match in the streets with their mates or girls twirling a skipping rope that was stretched right across the road. A line of girls would wait to 'run in' or three or four girls would jump together, all chanting their rhymes and skipping ditties at the top of their voices.

My husband and I visited the Black Country Living Museum during the summer with some friends and there were quite a few primary schools visiting that day. It made me smile to see all the children lining up on a cobbled street for a lady in period dress. She was holding a skipping rope with the other end tied to a lamppost and the children ran in, skipping and jumping the rope, squealing with laughter. Others chanted the number of skips each one managed. One or two tried to run in but were not very successful. If that sounds like a criticism, it's not meant to be. Children today have so many modern things to do that skipping, even if it's a game not lost, is a pastime not played that often. I know children still skip at playtime at school, but we skipped all the time. Three or four girls got together or even alone in the streets. We were all experts! Double ropes were sometimes used, and it would be ages before one of the skippers was caught out and you could be relieved of rope twirling.

Children today are no different now to how we were, once exposed to games that we played constantly years ago. Constant, unsupervised outside play was a given for children of our generation. Fears from increased traffic and other dangers have sadly put a stop to this…

Ilkeston Junction, just a few hundred yards down the road from us, was a little community all on its own, on the other side of the Erewash bridge. It was a hardworking, close-knit community who were generous with what they had, even if that might have been very little at times. Set alongside the railway station with the station master's house on the platform were scores of back-to-back terraced houses over four or five streets. I used to attend the Methodist chapel, along with many of The Junction and Station Road children and the anniversary parade went around The Junction streets, all of us in our new dresses and best suits.

Some of the terraced houses were very nice, most of the houses have now been replaced by factories. There was also a large hosiery factory called Meridian (now partly used by Armstrong Mills) where hundreds of girls and women and a handful of men were employed. There was also a pub called The Middleton, also known as (and now named) The Dew Drop Inn. The area also had its own little post office, a couple of corner shops, and of course a fish and chip shop; everything the community needed on a day-to-day basis. Oh, and Cossall pit was only a few hundred yards away.

Ilkeston Junction seemed to have giant everything on their playground! Their rocking horse seemed bigger than other playgrounds, the see-saw was longer, and the roundabout seemed much faster. You had to be

Our Street

very brave to go down and play on that playground if you didn't belong to the neighbourhood, though. The kids were very tough, and you would soon be challenged if you were an outsider and perhaps even get 'bashed up'. The lads around us wouldn't go down to use the playground unless it was with mates who happened to be one of the 'Junction kids'. We had a foot in both camps.

My grandma and grandad, at the time, still lived on Wentworth Street where their children (my dad, his brother Ken and sister Barbara) had been brought up. My Mam and dad had lived there for a short time too when they were married. A free pass to play wherever we wished!

What more could a child ask for?

CHAPTER 6

Dressing Up

In the forties and fifties, and even into the sixties, many parts of the country were still pretty rundown and people didn't have much by way of material things. Wages were low and rationing was still in force for some items into the 1950s. Even so, we would always have a good Christmas; there never seemed to be a shortage of food at our house. Mama seemed to spend the whole year preparing food for the weeks and months ahead: baking, pickling and bottling, preserving whatever was possible. She took advantage of each season's bounty to add to our table. She was a brilliant cook and a great planner, even for her generation. I loved her dearly and still think of her often…

Our Christmas presents were in no way comparable to what youngsters get today; and in no way comparable to what our parents told us that they recei-

-ved, such as an orange and a penny, perhaps some nuts or something similar.

My sister once had a brand spanking new bike bought for her. She had already spotted it, whilst pulling faces at me through the window during my piano practice, in the front room. It was hidden behind the piano and thought to be safe from prying eyes, seeing as she wasn't allowed in the front room (spared from having to study music.) It came with a year's warranty but, unfortunately, it didn't come with extras - such as road sense or a natural ability to stay upright. Not to be too unkind, I think it fair to say she was a menace to herself and to other road users.

After a fall, she gave up on it saying that there must be something 'not right about it.' We all had our own thoughts about that statement. Our dad took it over and, even though it was too small for him, he happily pedalled to work on it for years. She never tried again until middle age. Even then she

My Sister and I Dressing Up © 1946

had a bad fall on her first trip out and finished up having a long walk home. That bike quickly disappeared after its short ride, never to be replaced.

I, too, had a nice bike bought for me. It was very big and heavy, and it lasted me years. It even went away on the train to college with me in the guard's van. I was not too worried about it getting scratched as it was pretty old and second-hand when I got it, but it did have a brand new bell on it!

Annuals and art materials for me would be joyfully received at Christmas time. My 'Rupert' annual was read very sparingly as I attempted to control the urge not to keep reading and gobble it all up in a couple of days. I had been looking forward to receiving it all year, so I'd try to make it last as long as possible. Then it would be read and re-read countless times throughout the coming year. All my books were saved over the years, along with my artwork, including my portfolio of work from art college, along with brushes, frames and materials, all stored carefully away in the attic. Until one mad day my dad decided to help out with the kids collecting for bonfire night and donated the lot! I was enraged and could have wept (I did); no one even went into the attic all year. I still grit my teeth thinking about it.

Christmas passed all too soon before we were into a brand-new year. We would revert to our normal amusements, one of which was dressing up. My sister and I could happily spend most of the day doing so, not that we had much in the way of dressing up clothes. Much of our old clothing was recycled in some way or another. Those ways seem to have stuck with some; many is the time I go to throw something or other away and my husband says, 'no save that it, might come in handy!'

The result? Junk lies in the shed, in the loft or baskets in cupboards for years, never to be used. Many people who lived in those times, I suspect, would have difficulty with the throwaway society that we live in now.

Like most kids then, Mam's shoes would be borrowed. Well girls did anyway, we were inventive. She had two pairs; our coats would be tied backwards around our waists with their sleeves, and we were ready to go to the ball! We would have a little picnic, and imagine we were at a posh dinner in the back yard and our little dog Dinky was always part of our games.

He was very patient with us and didn't mind being dressed up at all. Mam was always cleaning, or washing and ironing and you kept from under her feet if you had any sense! But we only had a small back yard and there was nowhere to go to get out of the way really, and you would be very lucky to continue your game before it was interrupted by a, "Betty, do this" or "Betty, do that" and you didn't backchat your parents or say 'I'm not', in those days. You wouldn't have dared.

Not that our parents were heavy-handed, not like the tales some of our friends would tell of their parents. But our Mam had a tongue that could be as cutting as a cat o' nine tales if she was crossed or upset, when she was younger. I think their generation of woman were soon worn down with childbirth and constant drudgery in the home.

We were sent out on to the streets to play most days when not at school, unless the weather was really bad, and you were glad to get out. You didn't want to stay in or you would definitely have been given something to do. The steps and windowsills had to be rub-stoned every day, whatever the weather. There was always some job that needed to be done. By some of us anyway, did I mention my sister was allowed to say, 'I'm not'...?!

CHAPTER 7

Chaucer School
1940s - 1950s

Chaucer Infant and Junior School was where all the children from the Station Road area went. It was split into three parts - a nursery section, the girls' section on the Chaucer Street side and the boys' section on the Cranmer Street side.

It was a big school with several hundred children attending and like most state schools of that era it was pretty strict and regimented. A bell rang to mark the end of playtime or to start the day and everything stopped dead, not a sound. Then a whistle would blow, and everyone would hurry to their various form files, and process into assembly, or to their various rooms, all in silence.

When all the girls were out in the playground playing their different games, the noise from them all was pretty terrific, with the boys out on the other side of the building in a separate playground, adding to the din. Miners, many of whom lived in the terraced houses surrounding the school, would be working shifts and would be in bed during the day. It must have been something of a relief for some of them when that bell went, and the noise stopped. They must have got used to it, if they were anything like our dad, because after a shift down the pit he was that dog tired he wouldn't have noticed a bomb going off!

He was always up at the crack of dawn even when not at work. If my sister and I tried to stay in bed a little longer at the weekend though, he would be down in the kitchen early in the morning banging on the ceiling with the broom handle, 'Come on, let's be having you,' he would shout, 'do you know what time it is?'

'Yes,' we would think, 'blooming early! Leave me alone!' Bang, bang, bang went the broom handle on the ceiling.

Miss Hawley was the headmistress, and she was very strict; you would tremble if she wanted to see you - well, I would, being a little nervy. Her sister was also one of the mistresses. My Mam was once taking a net curtain down and replacing the garden cane being used for a curtain rod. "Here", she said, handing me the cane, 'take this to your teacher and ask her if she can use it.' Being a naïve girl, and used to doing whatever I was told, I took it and presented it to my form teacher. 'My Mam said can you use this', I said, proudly handing her the cane.

'Oh, how kind of her, Betty,' she replied, 'hold your hand out - you can be the first to try it.' It was a shock. I closed my eyes and held my hand out but she had a sense of humour and only gave me a token tap. When I went home and told Mam, she laughed and said, 'serves you right you daft 'apeth, I didn't really mean for you to take it, now get it back I need it for this curtain!'

The caretaker, Mr Horridge, always seemed to be shovelling coke down the stoke hole which was used to heat the school (not very well), blithely ignoring the screaming, shouting girls racing madly around him.

It was a good school, and we were treated well, mostly, by the female staff. I was glad to have been born a girl at that time though and to attend a girls' school.

It was quite legal and normal for teachers and parents to beat their children within reason, and many did.

Not in our house though. Our dad was a softie, although Mam's tongue could be like a cat o' nine tails when she lost her temper. Once a year the local newspaper, The Pioneer, would display awful NSPCC photographs of children from all over the country in their shop window at the bottom of Bath Street; children who had been so badly beaten they had to be taken into care. Those images would be thought far too graphic to show today's public. I remember looking at them with dad and he would shake his head and say, 'Those poor, poor children.'

Chaucer Girls 'Playtime' © 1949

CHAPTER 8

Chaucer Girls School Dinnertime

Many of the children at Chaucer Girls looked forward to dinnertime; they relied on it for their one good meal of the day. We got milk every day and the school dinners were quite nice. The teachers helped serve the dinners and you were not allowed to leave saucy plates. The only way to clear something from your plate if you didn't like it was to slip it in your pocket or wrap it in your hankie and tuck it into the leg of your knickers, which could be pretty messy if it was covered in gravy.

The teachers were very good at Chaucer Girls, compared to other schools in the area. About the worst thing you would get was a good slapping from the teacher, but on the other hand, they had very sharp tongues, and took no nonsense from anyone.

Chaucer Girls Dinnertime

People in Ilkeston of my parents' and grandparents' generations had an abundance of larger-than-life characters that were well-known throughout the community. This type of person rarely emerges nowadays, mainly due to the changes from the insular society of yesteryear, where much of their lives intermingled with each other. This contrasts with our global society today, where often people do not even know the names of neighbours living a few doors away.

However, one such person from my generation did emerge, and will long be remembered by generations of Ilkeston children and adults.

I am, of course, talking about Dorothy Haywood, who has sadly passed away.

I had known Dorothy (as many had) for most of my life. Dorothy was born and lived all her life on Flamstead Road, would have sat at the tables in my picture and was on duty there later, no doubt. When she left for her secondary education, she passed her eleven-plus and went to Hallcroft

School. She left Hallcroft and trained as a nursery nurse, and when her training was completed, returned to Chaucer. It was as if she had never left and there she stayed until her retirement. Dorothy was a kind and gentle lady but a lady who firmly and kindly guided her young charges into school life. Her distinctive voice made her a natural and mesmerising storyteller for children. She never really left Chaucer; she was still in demand even after her retirement. Dorothy will be missed and remembered by thousands.

My husband was born opposite Dorothy on Flamstead Road. He and his mum were living with his mum's sister and family whilst his dad was away at war.

He recalls his mum and aunt saying that Dorothy was knocking on the door asking if she could take the new baby for a walk, as she did for his cousins, the day after he was born, and she was only 6 or 7 years old herself. Dorothy's calling in life was always in her from the very beginning, I think.

Dorothy's father was also well known in Ilkeston and pictured in many mayoral processions as the Mayor's Mace Bearer and Dorothy cared for him until he died.

CHAPTER 9

Coal Delivery Day

Coal delivery day was usually a day to be dreaded. Miners were allocated a delivery of a tonne of coal every five weeks (which was part of their wages). The problem was it was just dumped in a heap outside your house, and you were responsible for getting it in. If you came home from school and saw a load of coal dumped outside the house your heart would sink because you knew how the rest of your day was going to be occupied!

Mounds of it had to be shovelled down the cellar and as much as you could cram into the coalhouse and through the yard. Families who only had one coal house and a length to walk down the entry had the worse job with the coal house needing to be boarded up to get it all in. Nobody surrendered their coal - no matter how much you had – it was too valuable. If you were caught selling it, or even giving it away though, you would lose your coal

Holmes family Blake Street, getting the coal in. circa 1951

rights, and possibly get the sack. Despite this we were always told by our dad to carry buckets of coal to the pensioners and widows in our street too. My dad was always very kind and liked to 'see them right.'

I think it must have been the law that it couldn't be left outside during the night. It seemed to be at our house, anyway, as the orders were that the endless mountain of black stuff had to be shifted the same day. It was usually our dad who ended up doing it but if he was working it was Mam who had to do it. If we saw it outside when coming home from school we tried to disappear or make a long detour, only to be faced with cries thereafter of 'where have you been 'til this time? Get a bucket!' when we finally showed our faces.

If dad wasn't home then Mam had to do it, and anyone else who was around would be roped in to assist with hauling it in. She would be not very ably assisted by my sister and I (if we had been stupid enough to be collared). Every little bucketful, though, helped to reduce the heap. None of us liked it; as well as being very tired when we finally finished, we were also covered in coal dust which was never fun with the prospect of a 'wash-down' at the sink.

My dad was once spotted going past the top of the street on a bus when he should have been returning straight home from work to help get it in. He ducked down as the bus was passing and he noticed the delivery had arrived but was spotted! We all knew the times the buses passed when the shift knocked off and were watching for him. He swore that it wasn't intentional and that he had honestly dropped something at that moment and didn't see the coal, but nobody believed him!

He never heard the last of it for the rest of his life. Any argument and up came that 'old potato'! If they read this book in heaven he will groan and say, 'Oh no! Not that again. Give it a rest!'

My Mam wasn't one to forget a 'slight' or an insult, even if it was often imagined. In their later years I once called in to see if they were okay. My Mam was sitting at the table watching a quiz programme on her portable TV. My dad sat practically next to her watching the news on the main TV, both with the volume at full blast! It was 1984, the miners on the picket lines on the news were chanting, 'Scab! Scab! Scab!'

'Yes,' Mam said 'and that's what your dad was – a scab!' My family had nothing, not even a slice of bread sometimes.'

'Oh yes,' said dad, 'whereas we were in clover. We had a coach and four horses outside to take us to school. You don't know what you're talking about!'

'I'm talking about scabs,' retorted Mam.

'Right,' I said, 'I'm off!' And I left them arguing bitterly about the strike... the 1926 miners' strike, that is!

Although a lot of our neighbours were miners, not everyone was. At that time there was plenty of employment in Ilkeston and everyone seemed to go to work. Bath Street would be pretty deserted in the daytime throughout the week.

Fuel was just as expensive for people back then, as it is now, and with no central heating, double glazing or insulation in houses, a lot of folk would say 'Eskimos were warmer in winter in their igloos.'

One young lad from a non-mining family, who lived on Flamstead Road, had a novel way of helping his family to keep warm. He would stand out of sight inside the cemetery gates and wait for the coal lorries coming from Cossall Pit. In the forties and fifties, they were old lorries (everything was worn out after the war.) If you stood at the cemetery gates you could hear the lorries turn off Station Road and painfully labour in first gear up the bit of a slope that is Alvenor Street. Picking up a bit of speed on the flat of Flamstead it would have to slow again to a crawl to turn the bend at the cemetery gates. It was at this point the boy would spring into action, positioning himself in the driver's blind spot with a big stick in one hand and a bucket in the other. He would leap behind the tipper lorry, which always had a poorly fitting tail gate, and then, 'WHACK! WHACK! WHACK!' The boy would bang on the tailgate and a shower of coal would fall out. As quick as a flash he would scoop up the coal and be away home, with the driver none the wiser that he had been gently mugged. He would soon be back for another lorry! I lived on the other side of Station Road and only ventured into that territory when going to school and never witnessed this.

My husband, who was born on Flamstead Road, saw this on many occasions back in the day and seemed to think that this 'young lad' still lived in Ilkeston. He's not quite so 'fleet of foot' these days, he says, and would probably not fill many buckets if he had to chase those old lorries today!

CHAPTER 10

Anniversaries in Ilkeston 1940s and 1950s

Anniversary days were one of the big occasions of the year right across the country, and Ilkeston was no exception.

Hundreds of people would turn out to watch anniversary parades, which were called Whit Walks across the country, but we just knew them as Anniversary Sunday.

Our chapel was opposite the Ilford Social Club, on the corner of Rupert Street, attended by many children from the Station Road and The Junction area. We would all gather there on the Sunday morning for the big anniversary parade. It was one of the few occasions parents could show off their children, and they all tried their best. We would all be in our Sunday best for the parade. Many of the girls would have new dresses, most of which were made at home, and those would only be worn in the evening.

We were Methodists and the sun was always shining for our parade. I think we must have had friends in high places. We went three times that day: the big parade in the morning, which was a procession around all the local streets, chapel after dinner and again in the evening.

The band would lead, rousing music playing, the big drum thumping its rhythm. The chapel's banners, held up proudly by some of the bigger children, would stand tall behind the band, followed by the older children, graduating down to the smallest ones and the helpers bringing up the rear.

Hundreds of people lined the streets and people would be hanging out of bedroom windows to get a better view. Excited kids and mothers, some pushing prams and pushchairs, would follow the parade all the way round, proudly watching their offspring.

Then it was chapel in the afternoon and evening. We all sat in tiers (with sometimes tears) and the chosen ones would stand up in front of the congregation and recite their poem, sing, or quote from the bible.

It was pretty terrifying. We would have been practising for weeks, and on the day, watching the congregation file in, your mind would go completely blank, and sometimes you badly needed the toilet. Some parents were there for all three sessions. Our dad used to sit on the fence by the Ilford Social Club, opposite the chapel, in the afternoon to give us moral support. We could see him if it was hot and the chapel doors were left open, our dog Dinky sitting patiently at his feet. Mam and dad would then go in the evening.

They were very happy times. All the teachers and helpers were kind and gentle, they told us stories, we sang, produced drawings and were taught good values, and sometimes we were taken on outings.

What's not to like?

Methodist Anniversary © 1950

Looking back, I suppose, we were pretty tough kids living in a tough area, always out playing and getting into scrapes. Usually, there were gangs of children in the streets or fields all day long when not at school; you were never short of friends.

Although most of our parents were kind and loving, we weren't brought up in a 'touchy-feely' society. There were boundaries at home and at school and if you crossed them, it was not counselling you could expect in those days.

To go to Sunday School was to go to a different world, gentle and calm. I loved it. The one thing I can't remember is any kind of religion or dogma being pushed at you; just a warm, gentle, friendly gathering every Sunday morning.

I think the widespread practice of anniversaries and parades began to die out across the country in the late fifties or early sixties. A shame, but times change.

CHAPTER 11

Ward's Butchers

We used to buy our meat from Ward's butchers on Station Road, on the corner of North Street. Ward's was a very well known shop in Ilkeston.

There was a cow's head made of stone above the door that I have put into the painting, unfortunately it finished up looking like a pig's head.

Ward's was a very good butchers shop, and very busy. One of the reasons he was busy, apart from the excellent meat, was the fact that he was known to give value for money. Mr Ward was known locally for his very tasty sausages; he would often cut one in half when weighing up and pop it into his mouth, something probably noted by housewives who would think it a good recommendation.

North Street.

The shop stood at the bottom of North Street, nearly opposite the Erewash pub, all gone now, of course, to make way for the relief road. I believe the cow's head that sat above the shop survived the demolition and is now kept by the Ilkeston Museum.

Starr's pawn shop was on the opposite side of the road. This was also a very popular shop. Articles could be sold and bought back later, when the customer had scraped together enough money to redeem their property. Austerity might be a modern term but many in Ilkeston had known all about austerity long before the word started being used. Everyone knew what kind of a shop this was, because pawn shops traditionally had three balls over the doorway.

Just up North Street, from the corner where Ward's stood, was Arial Pressings, a large factory, where workers would sweat the hours away on piece work. When the workers all turned out, there seemed to be hundreds of people rushing about, especially at lunch time, when all the factories and schools that were in the area took their break at the same time.

Midland General blue and cream double decker buses would queue up outside factories to take the workers to lunch and would return forty-five minutes later after picking them up and returning them to the factories. Single decker, half cab buses used to park down the side of the Erewash Pub on North Street to service Kimberley and Swingate.

Godbers, another kind of meat shop, stood on the corner of Chapel Street and Bath Street with the exterior of the shop tiled with dark green tiles. Godbers was the kind of shop you wouldn't see on our high street nowadays. It sold condemned meat for pets. Each piece of meat had green paint or dye on it to signify that it was condemned.

That shop was about the only shop in Ilkeston that I never entered. I would hurry past it from early childhood. The stench coming from it would turn my stomach. Its smell was probably no different from other butchers shops I passed but the word 'condemned' and the green paint on the meat in the window sent my imagination into overdrive.

CHAPTER 12

"Never, never talk to strangers…"

Once, during our school holidays, I had arranged with two friends to go on a bike ride and picnic to Stony Clouds which is situated the other side of Stanton Ironworks near to Sandiacre. We had been excitedly planning the ride for some time and had arranged to set off soon after breakfast as it was some distance away.

I packed a couple of sandwiches and filled a bottle with water for the journey and was packing my bag when Mam said, "where are you off to?"

'We're going on a bike ride,' I replied.

'Oh good,' said Mam, 'be careful, don't talk to any strangers and pack a sandwich for your sister because you're taking her with you.' 'Noo! We can't, it's too far for her', I cried, close to tears. 'Well go somewhere nearer and don't be late back for your tea,' she said.

This was her idea of being reasonable.

'You've got to take me,' my sister said, smiling. I could have wept.

While we had a freedom unimaginable by today's children, the downside was that the older ones usually had to look after their younger siblings all day, and there were a lot of big families in those days. Luckily (relatively speaking) I had only one chain around my neck, which was more than enough. It explained why we never strayed far from Johnny's (Wash Meadow) with its amenities to occupy them.

Upon meeting, my two friends looked upset. 'What have you brought her for? She can't come!'

'You've got to take me,' my sister said with her winsome smile. Usually this got her what she wanted, but it cut no ice with my friends.

'Can't we put her somewhere 'safe' like we did last time?' my friend said (another tale for another time, perhaps…)

The smile vanished from my sister's face.

'No, I daren't,' I said, 'I didn't half catch it for that.'

We set off with my sister, trundling happily behind us on her brown three-wheeled bike, ringing her bell and yelling, 'slow down! I'll tell me Mam if you don't wait. You've got to wait for me, our Bett!' as my friends sprinted ahead wanting to put some distance between us.

It was a fair distance of about five miles and hours later, it felt, we passed through Stanton Ironworks which seemed to go on forever. Big sheds skirted both sides of the road still coated with camouflage paint used to hide them from the aeroplanes trying to bomb the ironworks during the war. Looking both ways we crossed the railway line going through the centre of Stanton against the main offices. We could hear the crash, bang of wagons being shunted together by the little steam shunting engine but were not able to see their whereabouts and I screamed at my sister to hurry up and cross. It was a single track that crossed the road and drivers just looked both ways when crossing. There were no gates as only the ironworks used it, I think.

By this time the novelty of the bike ride had well and truly worn off for my sister. It was much too far for a little girl on a tricycle, and she was whining that she couldn't go any further after a mile of leaving home.

Never speak to strangers

We managed to get there around lunch time. It was a blazing hot day and we were all so glad to sit in the shade and get out our sandwiches. We hadn't even finished eating when a man seemed to appear from nowhere and started chatting to us, asking us where we'd come from. He was very friendly but we did our best to ignore him, the rules having been drilled into us from the very first time we were allowed out either alone or with siblings or friends. 'Keep on 'corsy' and DON'T talk to strangers, and never, never go off with anyone you don't know.' Our Mam would add,

'and if anyone tries to grab you - kick them where it hurts.'
Unfortunately, she neglected to say where that was!

Giving up on us he moved on to my sister who was looking at bugs or
something in the grass and he asked her what her name was. 'My name's
Cynthia,' she replied, ignoring the mouthed words of 'shut up and come
here' from us all. I think there was a radio programme on a Sunday
afternoon around that time where a girl would say, 'my name's Cynthia' and
we would all laugh. But we weren't laughing that afternoon.

There was nothing menacing about him - he was just being very
friendly, maybe a little too friendly for adults of that time talking to kids.
Usually we were considered a bit of a nuisance, I suppose, with there
being so many about. It was all pretty scary for us. We were quite alone, and
far away from other people.

My sister had no hesitation in chatting to him (still the same, talks to
anyone!) We, by this time, were close to panicking. The boy with us had a
rope wrapped around his waist (the sort of things boys did all the time).
He tied one end to my sister's handlebars and the other to his bike.
We grabbed her and put her on her trike, and we were off within
seconds, picnic abandoned. My sister's three-wheeler had a fixed
cog which meant the pedals would still go around whenever the bike
moved. We went so fast she nearly fell off the back as she couldn't
keep her feet on them. Her legs were flailing around in the air and
the pedals were whizzing round as she shrieked like a banshee.

After we had covered a little distance and calmed down, my sister
decided that this was a much better way to travel and insisted on being
towed most of the way back with her legs up and, to be honest, it was
easier all round to stop her moaning and groaning!

She told Mam that she hadn't even finished her sandwiches before we
came back but even at that age, she had the sense not to mention a
strange man to Mam. Oddly enough that was the last bike ride she ever
joined us on and never asked again! It was the only time I'd been to
Stony Clouds, and I've never been back since.

CHAPTER 13

Mr Smith's Pigs

Mr Smith owned the corner shop at the top of Blake Street and kept two pigs in a sty down the Ropewalk. During and after the war, when

rationing was in force, some people kept pigs for the extra meat for their families. They would have to join a pig club and be granted a licence from the food ministry and were required to follow strict guidelines before the licence was granted.

I apologise if some readers recall the rules and regulations differently but my memory is hazy on this subject. There seemed to be so many and you heard these tales told so often that they often blended together!

If a licence was granted you could rear two pigs: one could be killed for yourself and the other one would have to be sold to the Ministry for addition to the nation's food supply.

They were not allowed, on pain of a jail sentence, to sell any part of the pig that they kept and were supposed to eat it all themselves. This was rather difficult given there were no fridges to keep the meat fresh and so it was often salted.

Many people did sell, trade or swap the meat for other forms of food such as eggs, which were also rationed. This was called 'black marketing' and you could be jailed for being caught or involved. Punishment was very harsh. The government was very strict with anyone caught. People, of course, did what they could to get a little extra for their families although you had to be very, very careful. A neighbour who wasn't doing it could very well 'shop' someone who was.

My aunt's husband, who lived in Cotmanhay, used to relay the time during the war when he was friendly with a local farmer who was illegally rearing pigs hidden in his cellar. He bought half a pig and, when it was ready for collection, went up on his motorcycle and side-car late one night when the blackout was in force to collect it. The farmer loaded the side of pig into his side-car, and they covered it with sacking, and he set off home. He had just turned on to the main road when the local police sergeant stepped into the road waving his flashlight for him to stop.

He was so frightened he stalled the bike and couldn't get it going. The sergeant told him he needed to get his defective front light fixed and then stood chatting with him whilst he took his spark plug out and cleaned it. Finally, saying goodnight to him, he drove away and returned home, badly shaken.

Telling the farmer later about his brush with the law the farmer laughed and said, 'I know all about it. The officer called in next day and told me, he knew where you had been and guessed what you had in your side-car covered up with sacks. You were pretty safe, though, as he had had the other half of that pig!'

My aunt's husband also bred giant Flemish rabbits, to be sold or bartered. He said he would dispatch them with the copper stick when they were fully grown. My husband was telling this tale to our son-in-law, who looked genuinely puzzled and asked why the stick had to be made of copper and looked bemused when we roared with laughter. A different generation!

Mr Smith was very protective of his pigs. If he saw any children around the sty, he would soon be shouting 'What are you lot doing?! I'll tan your backsides if you're tormenting my pigs!'

'No,' we'd reply, 'we've just bought some scraps for the swill.' 'Oh, that's okay then,' he'd say.

Some people said he loved his pigs more than his kids and cried when it was time for them to be taken away (the pigs.) The former wasn't true, but the latter may have been. His pigs were very well looked after. Schools and some factories followed this practice (I think Bennerley School did right up until the end of the fifties) incorporating the keeping of pigs as part of gardening lessons. With the rise in popularity of Forest School education in schools across the country, maybe one day the art of pig keeping will return.

Mr. Smiths Pigs

CHAPTER 14

The Miners'
Welfare Seaside Trip

During the recent lockdown our youngest grandson, Thomas, asked us if we could help him with a school project he was doing from home.

He wanted to know what holidays were like in the olden days! We sent him some old snaps that we had of the family, and I painted a picture and told Michael, my husband, what it was like for me and my sister. Unlike his family - who went away every year - we never went for a week's holiday. We went just the once on the miners' day trip. Our Mam would take my sister and myself on our Methodist Sunday School trips along with The Junction kids and we had some wonderful outings. So, our one and only miners' day trip, has remained as a vivid memory.

Eventually Michael managed to get my story written down, but pretty slow-

ly due to my speech problem. By the time we had finished our grandson had finished his project for school and sent it in, so it was a 'oh, I've finished it now, Mama, but thanks anyway. The old family pictures were good though!'

So here's my story of a trip to the coast, finally complete…

Once a year the Miners' Welfare would organise the annual trip for miners and their families to Skegness.

Many children would be lucky enough to go away for a whole week, once a year but it was not unusual for kids in our neighbourhood to only get the one annual day trip to the coast. In the case of my sister and I, we went with them just the once. Our parents were homebodies and not very keen to go away on holidays… not that we felt deprived in any way - we weren't.

We boarded the train at Ilkeston North Station. Scores of children and parents were waiting to board the train, grandparents too in some cases. Everyone was excited at the prospect of a day away from the daily 'same old, same old' (something I think we can all appreciate now during these difficult times.)

Kids were running up and down the corridors of the train, often sticking their heads out of the strap-controlled sliding windows that were in the narrow passages between the carriages.

'You're going to get your head knocked off if you keep doing that!' parents would repeatedly tell them, 'and if you don't, I'll knock it off for you if you don't pack it in and behave!'

It often ended with one of the kids screaming as they got a soot smut or cinder in the eye. It was all steam trains in the forties and fifties. Minutes later you would often hear, 'What did I tell you? Stand still!' as the injured eye was poked and prodded with a spit-soaked handkerchief.

On arriving at Skegness Station, boys would be waiting with their homemade soap boxes on wheels (or trolleys, as we called them) waiting to be employed by any arriving passengers who were down for the week. They would load their luggage onto the carts to be transported to their boarding house, usually for about sixpence, which was about two and a half pence. No luck with us; we had only our sandwiches, macs and buckets and spades.

As we walked through the town, I was amazed by all the shops and the music and noise coming from the arcades and the streets thronged with people. We walked down to the seafront altogether as we had travelled down on the same train. Some mothers and fathers were darting in and out of the group trying to stop one or two of their kids from escaping into the arcades.

I was even more amazed when we got to the beach. I couldn't have imagined it without having actually seen it! The beach was packed when we got there, with what seemed like hundreds of people, all sitting or lying on towels and deckchairs. There were people threading their way between all the bodies to try and find a spot to settle.

Even though it was boiling hot, many of the men never took off their jackets and would sit in a deckchair, perhaps with trousers rolled up a little and ties still on and later sporting a handkerchief knotted at each corner placed on the head to protect their bald spots from the hot sun.

Children were making sand pies and exotic castles. They were happily running back and forth to the sea, which looked to be about half a mile away, to fill the moat of their castle with water. Their return journey often resulted in a show of anger, having got back to find someone had destroyed their creation.

Dads would be flying the kids' kite that had been bought especially for the day, while the children waited impatiently. They would mither for him to let them have a go, usually with them being told by their father to pick it up and throw it in the air for him to tug at the string to get it flying for them. This often resulted in him saying, 'you can have it in a bit!' when they eventually had it flying. 'Let him have a go!' mum would shout but dad was the expert (or so he said) and had to be allowed to have his fussy out of it.

We set up a windbreak with deckchairs behind it, sheltering us from the

stiff breeze that was blowing in from the sea. We looked with envy at people who were there for a week. Many had rented a chalet at the top of the giant steps built further along the beach, where we had moved to, which had been built to break up the crashing waves as the tide came in.

'They must have a bob or two,' Dad muttered.

Kids would come straggling in, shivering from splashing about in the sea; heavy woollen hand knitted costumes would often be dragged down to the knees with the weight of water trapped in the wool!

Women and girls were struggling to dress or undress with a large towel wrapped around them from neck to ankle, struggling with their clothing and shrieking if the towel fell or was pulled away by someone, the occasional bare bottom revealed to roars of laughter.

Sandwiches were unwrapped along with bottles of Tizer and other types of pop. Usually it was egg sandwiches for most of us - soggy with the heat - but still eaten ravenously thanks to the sea air. Everyone seemed happily oblivious to the fine sand particles blowing across the beach and sticking to the sandwich.

Some of us older kids were lucky and were allowed to go to the High Street by ourselves where the arcades were. Here we could play on the penny slot machines.

Some boys were taking it in turns to share a quick peep into a machine to see what the butler saw, while someone turned the handle to make the figures move. I was glad I hadn't wasted my penny. He didn't seem to see much at all from their accounts and it seemed more pennies always needed to be fed in just as it got interesting.

Pennies would be pushed into slots and ball bearings would be sent clattering around all the cups set there to catch them before being quickly lost at the bottom, missing them all.

Candy floss and sticks of rock were bought by those who had resisted the arcades. The noise, the crowds! How exciting it all was.

There was a constant stream of kids, back and forth, from the beach to the glass ceilinged underground toilets in the High Street, which was a bit of an adventure in itself. Going down into the loud, echoing room with crashing doors was a little like how I imagined a prison would be.

All too soon it was five o'clock and everyone started packing up. We had to get back to the station for the train which left promptly at 6.00pm. Anyone not there would be left behind.

Some mothers were in a state of sheer panic as one or two of their brood were found to be missing. Mams, dads and relatives were rushing around the beach frantically calling them. 'Just you wait 'til you get home!' must have been threatened a hundred times that day. One last trip to the toilets as we passed on our way to the station, or a 'Are you sure you don't want to go?' Everyone always seemed to make it back on time though.

By the time the train pulled into Ilkeston, exhausted youngsters were carried by mum and dad who were already festooned with bags, buckets and spades. The older ones were told to carry their own stuff!

Everyone agreed it had been a brilliant day and promised to do the same next year, God willing.

We were easily pleased in those days, and the sun always seemed to shine for us. Or am I wearing those rose-coloured specs again?

Mind you, it couldn't have been thought of as that brilliant by our mam and dad because we were never taken on the miners' trip again (or perhaps I missed something that happened that day as I merrily fed the penny arcade slots!)

CHAPTER 15

Johnny's

At the bottom of our street called Meadow Street which led onto a large meadow, officially called Wash Meadow. This was more commonly known by the locals as Johnny's. The meadow bordered the allotments, which have now gone and it has, for a long time, just been an embankment down to the side of the canal. How it came to be called Johnny's I have no idea, perhaps someone knows.

I read somewhere, a long time ago, that miners would play a game there, that consisted of a pile of stones with a special topping stone called a duck. The challenge was for players to take turns trying to knock the top stone off and that was where the saying to 'knock your duck off' came from. True or not I don't know, I've probably got it all wrong, hopefully someone will put me right. I would be interested to know.

Wash Meadow (Johnnies)

On Johnny's stood a playground for all the children of the area and to say that it was widely used would be an understatement. It literally swarmed with kids sometimes on the playground and spread across the meadow when they couldn't get on the swings and roundabout or 'Bobby's Helmet' as it was known. They would be racing about playing an assortment of games. Girls would spread bricks up against the far walls on one side of the meadow to simulate houses and would play happily for hours, with tins and suchlike used as kitchen utensils and dandelions as 'food'. The Bobby's Helmet was a great favourite with everyone, with lots of kids piled on; you could really get it spinning and rocking. I don't know whether they are allowed now but I am guessing they are probably classed as too dangerous for children.

I never knew anyone who was seriously hurt by these roundabouts though; you learned to hang on tight from an early age. The older ones were tasked with looking after their younger siblings and would hang on with one hand whilst clutching their brother or sister with the other. The swings were very tall and you would sit on the seat and sprint until you went so high - with your heart in your mouth - that the chains would go slack and instead of swinging you would drop with a jar to your spine sometimes with two on the seat, one sitting astride the other.

Whenever I pass now, along the Millership Way, I look across the road as we pass Johnny's at the always-deserted meadow with the two little rocking horses sat looking rather forlorn and lopsided on springs, and two slides for infants. I feel rather sad, thinking of the happy times thousands of kids have had on there over the years.

With few toys to play with, imaginative play was high on the agenda.

I had an older friend, her name was Joan Flinders, later Willis, and we spent many hours playing together.

Joan died some years ago but she wrote a poem about our tin bath and it was published in the Ilkeston Advertiser years ago. I came across the cutting in a book recently and thought how apt it was. I smiled when I thought of our tin bath from Blake Street. It had hung on the wall and was brought home by my husband saying, 'it might come in handy.' And so it did.

Our daughter and her best friend used it exactly as we did all those years ago at the top of our garden. Until, that is, our daughter decided that it was cruel to keep Goldie, her goldfish, in his little bowl any longer. He had happily swum round and round in his bowl for years in the kitchen but she thought that we should have a garden pond and that Goldie should be re-housed. So, one Saturday morning the tin bath was sunk up to its rim in the garden, a few pond plants put in to make Goldie's new home nice. We were going up in the world at last; we now had a garden pond. Goldie was introduced to his new home the same day (probably traumatised after his little bowl.)

On the following Sunday lunchtime we sat in the living room and saw our neighbour's cat sauntering casually through the drive gates with Goldie hanging from his mouth. B.B.C was his name (Big Black Cat) and we frantically chased him down the road and up into his own garden where he disappeared under a hedge. Goldie was never seen again. My daughter went into mourning and blamed her father for not making our new fish-pond cat-proof. Our new pond was dug up, the bath slung behind the shed but years later rescued by my son who took it to his house to use as a holding tank whilst he cleaned his own fish pond.

So, to this day our old tin bath (now hanging in our son's shed) is still doing its stint.

In remembrance of my friend Joan.

The Old Tin Bath

Our old tin bath was a great delight
Not just used on a Friday night
Upside down as a table top
My friend and I would play at shop
Stones wrapped up in bits of paper
Bottles of water as lemonade
Broken biscuits all displayed
On our old tin bath.
Fed up with that we would fill it with water
Paddle in it and squeal with laughter
Out comes the water, now it's a boat
Our back yard was all afloat
Used for everything was our old bath
A stage for concerts, we would dance and sing
Oh what joy that bath did bring
Alas, no more, our old tin bath
With all that wear it started to dint
Never mind it had done its stint
Our old tin bath on our back yard.

Joan Willis née Flinders

CHAPTER 16

Ilkeston Swimming Pool 1950s

Ilkeston swimming pool was very popular with many people, young and not so young. The kids would go there in droves in the summer, and there would often be so many people in the pool, that you could only splash about.

If you tried to swim you would be bumping into someone every few strokes. It would only cost a few pence to go in for an unlimited time.

The cabins were very dilapidated before they were modernised and there were holes in the cabin sides, stuffed with bits of paper to stop boys trying to peep into your cubicle.

You would come back to your cabin for your towel and find about seven other piles of clothes in with yours and often you would go home with a

Ilkeston Swimming Baths, Mr. & Mrs Murden in charge. Circa 1950

frayed towel full of holes that had been left in place of your nice one or a scruffy vest in place of yours, much to your mam's fury.

Before you went into the pool, you would have to walk through the slipper bath full of chlorinated water to clean all the dirty feet. It was awful, cold and slimy from the scores of people who had gone through before.

The water in the pool was clear blue after its change once a week but by the end of the week it was so grey and murky you couldn't see the bottom. It was the best wash many of the kids got all week.

Mr and Mrs Murden, who were very strict, ran the pool, and they stood for no messing about.

Mrs Murden gave swimming lessons that were very effective. A halter would be tied around the pupil and he or she would be towed, usually the width of the pool. If you couldn't keep up, or your mouth was open and filling with water, hard lines. You soon learned to swim.

Mr and Mrs Murden were very well-known in the borough. They seemed to know the names of everyone, child and adult alike.

The baths were a major part of the town's social and school life in those days.

I believe Mr Murden drove the town's only ambulance during and after the war and their granddaughter is a local businesswoman and still lives in Ilkeston.

CHAPTER 17

Gunn's Toy Shop

Gunn's toy shop was the finest toy shop in the area. It was situated just above Jackson's, the large grocery store, on the corner of Stamford Street, opposite Pelham Avenue. Originally a paper and stationery shop, just below Marks & Spencer, Gunn's only stocked a few toys before it moved to larger premises where it remained until they closed.

The window displays the store owners set up in Gunn's were something else. Nearly all the shops in Bath Street at that time had a good window display and they took real pride in it. Jackson's even had professional dressers, who used to travel the length and breadth of the country, to dress theirs.

Gunn's didn't need to employ external people though, they were professionals.

Toys were arranged to maximise every tempting bit of space in the windows to full effect. Children, with their parents, would stand at the window just gazing at all manner of toys they could only dream about getting for Christmas. Families would come from miles around just to look in the window even if they could not afford to buy anything, although they did have a club that you could pay into to get that special something for Christmas.

Things were becoming easier, and the standard of living had improved, making items more accessible and more sophisticated toys were starting to be produced in the late fifties and early sixties.

During the first half of the 1950s toys were simpler – there were dolls and mini cooking and sewing sets for the girls. There was a prevalent 'let's get them prepared' attitude in those times which has thankfully changed!

Bikes, Dinkies, cowboy and army costumes and cap guns were always a favourite with the boys. Children used to have mechanical toys too, before the widespread introduction of the battery.

At Christmas, Gunn's would often rent a large room in the Rutland Hotel at the bottom of Bath Street to show off their best toys to maximum effect. Elaborate train sets were set up that ran all around the room, through model villages, with signals and stations along the track. Scalextric cars would also be whizzing round.

It was always thronged with men and boys longing to have a go. I think they missed a trick there; many of them would have loved to help set up the tracks and associated scenery if the interest showed in the exhibition was anything to go by. Perhaps they did…

A shop called 'Youngsters' opened at the top of Bath Street, opposite the old Argos shop. They sold quality toys and pushchairs for some time. In the late seventies, Fords opened halfway down Bath Street. They sold very cheap toys and many other things but with the decline of the lower end of the street, all those factors must have had a huge impact on Gunn's customer base.

Xmas Shopping at Gunn's Toyshop © 1953

My most enduring memory of Gunn's is not of the many beautiful toys purchased in that treasure trove over the years but of my husband and I standing, with our two-year-old son in his arms, looking into that magical window just before Christmas. Our son's waving hand then proceeded to hit his father in the eye, knocking out his contact lens. This was in the late 1960s and contact lenses were very expensive - around two weeks wages - and not quickly replaced.

Panic ensued and pedestrians were stopped! You can imagine the number of shoppers on a busy Saturday morning in the run-up to Christmas. He had shopping bags placed strategically trying to stop anyone walking on the pavement and stepping on the lens, whilst standing with one arm extended and a struggling child in the other.

A kind member of staff from Gunn's shop came out with a brush and carefully swept where we had been standing into a corner. I went down on my hands and knees, my bottom in the air and my nose about an inch from the pavement. Concerned and sympathetic shoppers peered at the pavement over my shoulder in a fruitless search for the lens, whilst my husband loudly directed me this way and that. In the end we had to give up, with the sheer number of people trying to get past making it an impossible task.

A couple of days later my husband arrived home all smiles - the lens had turned up from where it had been hiding… under his eyelid. I could have cheerfully, and very slowly, strangled him at that moment. I was not amused, my embarrassment still hotly felt. His cries of 'how was it my fault?!' cut no ice with me at the time.

Gunn's has sadly gone now. The store gave so much pleasure to so many people; children and their families had many a happy Christmas thanks to the beautiful toys discovered in there. What a huge wrench it must have been for the family that owned it and worked so hard for so many years, to close its doors for the last time.

CHAPTER 18

Fish, Chips and Batter Bits

Saturday was a great day. When we returned from doing the shopping on Bath Street and the market, my sister and I were sent for fish and chips.

'I can't carry any more than this,' she would whine. 'I'll drop them.' She'd then spend the next half hour or so wandering about, chatting to everyone, including the dog, whilst I would be stuck in the queue balancing a pile of basins and Cyn with one plate.

We thought Wortley's fish and chip shop on Station Road was the best in Ilkeston. While we waited in the seemingly never-ending queue we would stand or squat down watching Mr Wortley frying the chips through the window. A big pot of peas would be simmering on his gas stove at the back of the shop shop and a large 'pop' cabinet would be steadily emptying as we patiently waited. The helpers in the shop were all dressed in white overalls and Mr Wortly in a white apron. Everything in that shop was spotless.

The business only closed fairly recently, and it seems a shame after goodness knows how long.

Mr and Mrs Wortley owned the shop for years. It was open lunch times and evenings and was a thriving business. There were quite a lot of fish and chip shops in Ilkeston up until the late sixties when they started to decline a little, especially the small back street ones. A once cheap family meal often called 'Britain's National Dish' started to become progressively more expensive.

All the shops had seemed to do well and make a decent living at that time; some had been there for many years. The most popular were the ones on the main streets, best placed to get the footfall, of course. A married couple used to own the shop opposite Woolworth's for a long time and there were always queues outside at lunch times, with workers and shoppers waiting for their lunch. The helpers would shout to people who were queuing up outside on Bath Street, 'Table for two, ready', or whatever was free. They would just do pie and mash on a Monday evening which was very popular. Customers would wait patiently and, when seated, they would either be chatting to complete strangers they had been seated at a table with or just ignore them completely!

The pace of work there was frantic. The wife would be serving non-stop behind the counter whilst her husband was frying as fast as he could. The two helpers would be dashing about bringing meals to the table, clearing dirty dishes away and wiping down ready to take the next order. They were all run off their feet in that very busy period at lunchtime.

'Styles', which was further up Bath Street, used to be just as busy. They were very well organised, and everything ran like clockwork. 'Briggs', a family business at the top of Nottingham Road, seemed to have been there forever. Saturday seemed to be fish and chip day for everyone in our neighbourhood and in the town. Friday, too, was a day when many across the country would only eat fish. It still is for many but nowhere near as many adhere to that tradition now.

It was a pretty demanding business to be in. Owners and employees worked hard from early in the morning. Piles of newspapers also had to be cut into squares for those people taking their fish and chips away open and not wrapped up and be put around the little greaseproof bag and paper that they went in. I would sometimes see Mr Wortley taking delivery of a load of potatoes when I was going to school in the morning. These all had to be washed and peeled. I used to be fascinated to see him put a potato on a device with a grill on it, pull down a handle and marvel as the potato was turned into chips that fell into a bucket. I would have loved to have had a go. I was easily amused!

People would often fetch their meals from the fish and chip shops with basins and baskets for the whole family and in those days, there were some big families. It felt as though every person in front of you in the queue carried bowls for at least six or seven people.

'Wortley's' also had a kid's room where you all sat on long benches at tables, served by a lady called Daisy. She also kept order when the children got too noisy and boisterous, which was often if they had to wait long for their dinner.

I never sat at that table, having to take all our family's fish and chips home. God forbid I got the order wrong and someone hadn't got their peas, or they had peas and didn't want them. When you got home after queuing for ages, they would all sit waiting for me to get back. I was always greeted with the same words every Saturday without fail from Mam. Not 'good girl' but, 'where have you been all this time? I bet they are stone cold now! Did you put plenty of salt and vinegar on like I told you?'

I'd reply with, 'No, Mam, Mrs Wortley sprinkled them before she wrapped them,' having had no chance to salt and vinegar them myself. 'Oh aye,' Mam would say. 'I just bet she did.' All the housewives of that period had eagle eyes for any skimping with rations or what they thought of as short measure in anything weighed. 'Half a pound? Never!' Mam would say about something she had sent me out for. 'I bet he had a finger on the scales when he weighed this!'

Wortley Fish & Chip Shop, Station Road.

'Can't you get a simple order right', Mam would say, 'and why aren't there any batter bits?' Mrs Wortley would sometimes sprinkle some fish batter bits on your chips if you asked, free of charge, but I never liked asking.

'She never asked for any again, Mam', my charming sister was more than likely to reply (always pulling laughing faces at me behind Mam's back if she had been telling tales.) 'Don't you touch her', Mam would say without turning round if I even as much as took a step towards her. My sister got to be quite an expert at winding me up.

My dad was an ARP warden during the war, and he used to say (often!) that he walked all the way to Hallam Fields one night to get my Mam fish and chips when she was pregnant. It was the only shop around Ilkeston open that particular night.

He told me fish and chips weren't rationed during the war but there were always shortages, and the shops often wouldn't open. He said when they had a delivery, they would put a big notice in the window saying, 'FRYING TONIGHT.'

The fish and chips that were to be wrapped up to be taken away were always laid on a clean sheet of paper and then wrapped up to be kept nice and warm between sheets of old newspapers. I dare bet diamonds, after that long walk across the bottom cut to Hallam Fields and back when my dad returned, she'd say, 'Where have you been all this time? I bet they are stone cold!'

CHAPTER 19

Bostock's Off-Licence

Bostock's 'Beer-Off' (as an off-licence was commonly known in this area) was alongside the gasworks on Rutland Street in Ilkeston.

It was very popular with the workers from the gas works and Town Station at the top of Rutland Street, for whom Mrs Bostock would make sandwiches or filled cobs.

The Bostock family were well-known to the people of Ilkeston. Mr and Mrs Bostock's son was the caretaker at Bennerley School for many years. Their grandson, Philip, worked at Ilkeston North Goods Depot and was tragically killed on the railway line off Derby Road in 1965 in a crane accident whilst working overtime one Sunday. They were a lovely and very hard-working family.

Beer-Offs were normal shops with an alcohol licence with a separate counter allowing them to serve alcohol. They could be found all over towns, often situated on street corners. Proper beer pumps would be behind the counter, and the shopkeeper would pump the beer from barrels situated in the cellar into jugs people brought to be filled. They would place a large funnel into the neck of bottles if they had no jug and I even saw people taking empty sterilised milk bottles with wire snap tops to be filled!

Some pubs would also have a little room, often with a little sign hanging over the counter saying, 'Jug and Bottle', where people could have their jugs filled to take home. They were incredibly popular with the older generation in the neighbourhood, especially women who wouldn't go into the tap room and in those times would not always have been made welcome if they had.

Perhaps some pubs still have that little room or a counter with a window that opens into the bar from the passage… I really don't know but I can't imagine there would be much call from ladies who liked their draught beer enough to go out with a jug now! With the advent of cheap alcohol in supermarkets and everyone fully embraced into the pub scene, I think that generation has probably died out.

Once people's jugs had been filled with beer, and if it was a fine evening, they would go home and drink it sitting on their doorsteps talking with neighbours. This was quite common in the summer months as there was no TV to keep anyone indoors and people mixed with their neighbours in a completely different way to nowadays.

Some liked to stand and drink in the entry alongside Bostock's 'Beer-Off'. The shop was always very popular when the pubs closed (which in those days was at ten o'clock) and groups of older men would buy their beer from Bostock's and congregate in the entry and street alongside the shop, reminiscing and telling tales from work or times past. Their chats and laughter could sometimes get rather noisy, much to the disgust of those walking by.

Walking down Rutland Street late one evening with my mam, after we had been to the pictures at the New Theatre, we would sometimes call into the chip shop on Rutland Street. With our fish and chips wrapped in newspaper we would walk down to cross over Johnny's (Wash Meadow to Blake Street.) She would put her arm around my shoulders and hurry past the group of men in the entry alongside Bostock's casting a disapproving eye at the group who were noisily roistering, their laughter echoing around us. The laughter would end abruptly and they would soon hurriedly disperse if they saw the local 'bobby' or, even worse, Sergeant Moon, approaching on his bike down Rutland Street!

Once the revellers had gone, you would often see the local beat bobby disappearing out of sight, up Mr Bostock's entry in the daytime for a cup of tea and a bacon sandwich and in the evening for a swift half and a packet of mints.

Everyone knew that the policemen had their regular places to drop in and have a cup of tea and a chat, or something a little stronger from a friendly publican or 'Beer Off' like Mr Bostock's. The trouble was, the sergeants and inspectors in charge of the shift knew the regular drop-in places too and would try to catch them skiving.

Sergeant Moon was feared by locals and police constables alike, who sometimes got up to no good. He could often be seen lurking in shop doorways trying door handles checking they were locked all night long, waiting to catch unsuspecting policemen out who were not doing their job or not being where they were supposed to be.

There were several sergeants in the Ilkeston police force, one for each shift, and they were all very strict. But it was Sergeant Moon, a big man, who had a name that seemed to be feared by all. He was an imposing figure, and he would often be seen glowering at groups of youths or young men he suspected of being up to no good, standing, holding his bike, with his heavy cape thrown across one shoulder. He was reputed to often swing and catch some unfortunate with the metal neck buckle and chain around the ear if any trouble arose and, having read the Advertiser, it often did on a Saturday night.

He was once standing behind the telephone box at the bottom of Alvenor Street, and he shouted at me to stop and accused me of not stopping at the halt sign on my bike. I had to walk home afterwards on trembling legs. Good job I only lived across the road.

I am still protesting my innocence to this day. I should have knocked his helmet off. Well, that's what I thought to myself when I was safe in my bed with Mama.

Unlike today, the only time you would see a policeman without his helmet or hat was when it had been knocked off in a scuffle. The helmet seemed, to me, to define their authority and which they all wore with pride.

CHAPTER 20

Doing a Runner

When I was growing up most people would only bathe once a week. The rest of the week a 'good wash-down' was the order of the day. Usually, Friday night was 'bath night' but some people went even longer. Whilst most of us would be pretty put out if we had to do that nowadays, it should be remembered that most terraced houses in those times had no bathroom. It was the tin bath in the scullery (if you had one) or in front of the fire if modesty wasn't a problem. As youngsters, none of us thought much about it. It was normal to us. That was just how things were.

It was a problem heating the water for Mam though. Saucepans would be heated on the stove, the copper laundry washing water would occasionally be used, or sometimes the copper used to heat the water up, especially for the bath. For this, a coal fire would have to be lit under the copper that was built into the side of the kitchen and the water would be bucketed into the tin bath. Most people who have used a tin bath will perhaps remember how fast the water cooled and would have to be topped up with a kettle of boiling water just to keep it hot.

On wash day I was plonked into the copper in the evening, into the still hot water that had been used for the washing that day and I could feel the bottoms of my feet all slimy with the soap of the day's wash.

We were more fortunate than most though. My grandma (Dad's mum) was the caretaker of Castledine's, the upmarket store at the bottom of Heanor Road, which is now a Citizens Advice Bureau. She lived in the flats behind the store. We would walk there every Sunday morning and use her bath with hot running water (what luxury!) Grandma would sometimes open the shop for us to wander round and look at all the lovely stuff inside. This was usually to bribe my sister into being a little more amenable…

The bath would be run for you. Even in the new council houses with bathrooms and a hot water tank heated from the back boiler of the coal fire, the same orders would be issued to the bather: 'don't use all the water!'

My young sister, Cynthia, wasn't a fan of the bathing procedure, wherever or however it was carried out. On the walk up Rutland Street Dad would warn her and say, without fail, 'You'd better behave this week, madam, or you're for it!' We never found out what she was 'for' because, unfortunately, she never got it. Dad was a softie. To say she was a pain would be putting it mildly. She didn't want a bath. She wasn't having a bath. But once in you couldn't get her out and, of course, I would have to have mine last which by the time we had finished with all the time-wasting and dramatics, Dad would be shouting to me to get a move on. 'Your Mam will have dinner ready,' he would shout. Unlike a lot of miners, he wouldn't be in the pub on a Sunday dinnertime. He was never a drinking man. He had a much more interesting hobby - one that had four legs, could run very fast and that took a lot of studying every day to guess how fast!

One Sunday morning we were off to Grandma's for our weekly bath. We opened the gate and started walking down the garden path when suddenly the back door flew open with grandma staggering out, coughing and choking, blood pouring from her mouth down her pinafore. Grandad was behind her, slapping her back and shouting, 'Are you alright? Are you alright?!'

Well, no, she wasn't, she was choking! She loved beetroot and, when cooked, she would often eat one warm like an apple. Unfortunately, a piece had gone down the wrong way and she'd choked. It was beetroot juice we were seeing, not blood. Dad rushed down the yard to try to help. We were rooted to the spot in horror. Well, I was, my sister had the 'screaming abdabs' and she was off! Shrieking like a banshee, she ran at top speed across the bottom of Bath Street and down Rutland Street, across Johnny's and all the way home. I swear we could hear her screaming her head off most of the way.

Once Grandma had recovered, Dad had to go and see if she had got home ok and I was left to have a deep bath in peace for once. When I got older I would use the slipper baths that were part of Ilkeston's swimming baths opposite the old police station. Mr and Mrs Murden were the superintendents. I knew them from swimming regularly from a very young age and got on well with them both. Mr Murden kept the slipper baths spotless, and there was no one shouting, 'Hurry up! Don't use all the water!'

CHAPTER 21

Coffins, Candles and Sanatogen Wine

The front room (or parlour) was used only on Sundays or special days by just about all working-class homes up until around the sixties. It was not even for Sundays in our house, but even so everything was polished daily, and the brasses and the fire irons were polished with Brasso once a week until they were gleaming (my job.) It was Mam's pride and joy. Only I was allowed in daily, for one hour's piano practise. I spent more time in that room than the rest of the household put together.

Needless to say my sister didn't have to go through this rite of passage but I would see her grinning face peeping through the window occasionally whilst practising.

Our house was lit with gas mantles until the late fifties or early sixties. The landlord needed his arm twisting even then to put electricity in and when it eventually was, Dad had more attachments to the single light fitting in the centre of the ceiling for various electrical items than you could shake a stick at! How nothing caught fire I'll never know…

We would all sit together in the living kitchen in the evenings, my uncles still living with us, listening to the wireless (powered by a battery called an accumulator.) The gas mantle would be hissing and popping, the coal fire would be burning brightly and casting flickering shadows around the room. 'Journey into Space', 'Dick Barton, Special Agent' and 'Man in Black' were popular radio programmes of the time, listened to by our family and most of the country. When these had finished, and if there was nothing else interesting on, we would sit and talk about our day. The adults might mention accidents that had happened at work or an event that was in the papers or perhaps there had been a murder trial that had been followed by everyone in the country, reported widely on the wireless and in the newspapers. If someone was due to be hanged for murder the next morning at 8am, I remember there would be comments like 'he won't get much sleep tonight' or 'he won't be hanging about much longer' and 'hanging's too good for him!'

Supernatural stories were told in hushed voices; our Uncle Ted was a master at telling these and I would sometimes go to bed in a state of terror. A little cruel really but we were not so 'touchy-feely' at that time and they found it amusing to scare us until Mama put a stop to it. 'Enough now! Pack it in, our Ted!' she would say. 'Too late Mama,' I'd think.

When the 8 o'clock 'pips' on the wireless went the next morning at breakfast before we went to school, Mama or Mam would say, of the condemned man, 'That's him gone now and good riddance too.' No sympathy for murderers.

When people died they would be laid out in the parlour and left in their open coffin for three days until the funeral. Neighbours would call in to see their deceased friend or relative for the last time and pay their respects. When a friend of mine died, Mam took me along to her house to see her. She lay in her coffin in the new dress that she had just had for our Sunday School Anniversary Day. She had died on or around her birthday, so they had put all her birthday presents in with her at her feet. It was very sad. It didn't distress me, but I can still recall every detail of that room as if I'd seen it yesterday. All the woman there around the coffin, one crying. Even down to a damp patch in the corner of the room. When we got home Mam gave me a glass of Sanatogen wine and she had a large one too. I was never taken to see anyone else. I think Mama had a word. I loved Mama dearly, she was a real mother hen. No wonder, though, that they used to give me Sanatogen wine daily for my nerves.

One day my Mama was taken poorly and had to lie on the sofa in the kitchen. One of her sons, my Uncle Ted, sent for an ambulance but Mama died suddenly as she was being put into it. The crew refused to take her saying she was logged has having died at home and Dad and my uncles would have to take her back into the house. The sight of my uncles and dad struggling to carry Mama up the street and through the narrow side door into the front room was imprinted on my brain forever. I was fourteen, with the emotional resilience, where my Mama was concerned, of a much younger child. It affected me deeply for a long time.

The awful scene would play back in my mind's eye for years.

She was laid out by Mrs Deering, a nurse at the Ilkeston Hospital and a neighbour, who performed that task for people. Mama was put into a coffin in the front room. My young sister was taken in to see her and told me, 'she looks beautiful with her hair plaited and her best nightie on.' I refused to go in to see her. I just couldn't believe she was gone forever.

Relatives would be calling, and they would go into the front room to see her, chatting to Mam and Dad and each other, having cups of tea and reminiscing about Mama as if she had been gone years and not just a day or so.

When my sister and I were going up to bed, with our candle casting giant shadows in the darkness of the hall at the bottom of the stairs, on the night before the funeral, Dad asked us, as we passed the front room with the door ajar, 'Would you like to go in and say a last goodbye to Mama?' We shot up the stairs like all the hounds of hell were on our heels. My sister, who had spent the day telling anyone who would listen how she hadn't been frightened at all, nearly tore the nightie off my back in her efforts to get past me. 'I didn't mean to scare them!' our dad protested to Mam when she told him off. He was a lovely dad, but I didn't believe him then, and looking back I still believe he wanted to get a reaction from us (he succeeded.) 'Give her some Sanatogen' he said, 'she'll be reyt.'

I loved my Mama dearly and had slept with her from being born. I had never slept without her beside me. That night, in bed, thinking of her alone in the front room in her coffin was the worst night of my life. I spent the night half-asleep, half-awake watching the door, half expecting it to open and Mama to be standing there in her best nightie. Losing her affected me deeply for a long time.

I flatly refused to go to the funeral despite a lot of pressure from Mam. I just couldn't bear the thought of what was to happen. Mama was in the Salvation Army. They were very kind and they held the service in our kitchen but it all seemed surreal seeing all these people, crowded into our little kitchen, with the captain in his uniform and his wife in her bonnet saying prayers and singing hymns.

My mum and dad's generation, and their parents before them, had been exposed to so much more horror, loss and tragedy than we generally are now. They grieved just as much then as we do today but many had lost babies, family member to illness and men to accidents and two world wars.

People also died much younger then. I think the general attitude taken was, 'it's sad but that's life.'

CHAPTER 22

Ilkeston Fair in the 1950s

Ilkeston Fair was, and still is, a time of great excitement. In the forties and fifties, old smoky, smelly engines would drive around the roundabouts and once there was a steam engine (I think - I spent so much time at 'the pictures' as a child, some old film might have merged with reality in my memories!) The country was still recovering from the war and 'make do and mend' was still much in evidence.

My mam and dad used to say that the Cake Walk was the same one that they had walked on as children and I told mine the same. It still looks and sounds the same but I've no idea just how old it actually is. The small stall holders would be selling hot mushy peas, shrimps and mussels served up in little pot dishes. Everyone would return them when they had finished eating to be washed and used again. Surprisingly, they never seemed to lose any to theft.

Ilkeston Fair © *1955*

The boxing booth was a great favourite. Situated opposite the Harrow Public House, great crowds of men (many of whom were accompanied by women) would pack the large tent. I have never been in a boxing booth so can only relay what I heard male members of my family re-telling what happened in there.

Just looking at the four or five boxers standing with their arms folded in front of the tent was scary enough, whilst the promoter exhorted the crowd gathered in front of the tent with, 'Come on lads, come and have a go with any in your weight range, all you have to do is stay on your feet for three rounds to win five pounds.'

They were tough looking men, with squashed noses, and cauliflower ears - true stereotypes. The lightweight boxers looked as if they needed a good meal and as though a strong wind might blow them over. They may have looked pretty easy to beat but from what my uncles said these men were very fast and skilled.

You wouldn't have thought so, but the booth did a brisk trade every night. Five pounds in winnings was quite a good sum in the fifties when, I suppose, the average wage was around ten pounds, so it must have been quite tempting to some.

My uncle used to say the best time to be outside the booth, was when the Harrow Public House across the road was turning out at 10.30. Young, tough miners with a belly full of Shippo's (Shipston's beer) and Dutch courage, egged on by their mates, would hold up their hands to volunteer and were quickly bundled into the back of the tent by assistants to be put into a boxing strip.

The fighters usually gave the crowd value for money, letting the would-be champ get within smelling distance of a fiver before planting him on his bottom! From what I was told, if the contender put up a really good fight the crowd would have a 'whip-round' for him even though he had lost. My uncle had a name for this practice, but I can't recall what it was.

Many a tough young miner or ironworker would come out with a black eye and a bloody nose, though, and no five pounds.

One young man, who I was told would often take on one of the boxers was a chap called Jimmy Featherstone, a local lad, who was a very good boxer. I don't know if he had been trained in the army or somewhere, but my uncle said he usually came away with his winnings. He said the booth owner wasn't bothered because the tent was always packed solid when this well-known character boxed. You could hear the roars from the men right up to the big wheel sometimes, and you knew there was a good fight on.

Jimmy lived on my mother-in-law's street, and she said what a nice chap he was, very sociable and friendly. Sadly, Jimmy died a while ago in his seventies. There were so many great characters around in Ilkeston at that time and it is sad to think that many of them are no longer with us…

As was the case most Sundays at our house we would have stewpot for breakfast. It would be in a big saucepan in the oven on the coal range, stewing nicely all night.

When you got up on the Sunday mornings after Ilkeston Fair and sat at the table with the gravy thin and the meat scarce, I would know that my uncles had been late coming in from the fair or pub. They'd been at the stewpot, watering it down to disguise their pilfering. They had no shame either, flatly denying any knowledge of the theft when Mam and Mama challenged them.

How times change. The thought of stewpot for breakfast and a big dinner at noon doesn't bear thinking about!

CHAPTER 23

The Truants

My sister hated school. Once, when she should have been at school, my dad went to get some coal and found her standing on top of the coal at the back of the coalhouse.

'What are you on with?' he said.

'Shh! Don't tell Mam,' she whispered.

So he shut the door and left her, saying nothing to Mam.

If she had been put into the coalhouse as a punishment (not that she ever was punished) for five minutes she would have screamed the street down. She could get away with anything and I could get away with nothing, being the eldest. She came in for her dinner at her usual time of about 12.30, having spent the morning in the coalhouse sitting on a heap of coal. She had her dinner, and then walked back to Cavendish School (now gone) in the afternoon, probably with some fabrication as to why she had been absent in the morning or perhaps a note from Dad, given she could usually talk him into getting anything she wanted.

She had Home Economics when she got back to school, made a nice stew and walked home, cutting through the cemetery as she often did. On this particular day she spotted the man who locked the bottom gates, walking on the pavement on the other side of the railings. He spotted her and it became a race, because he was a bit of a jobsworth and, without doubt, would have locked them if he'd got there first, forcing her to walk back.

Her jug full of stew was half emptied as it slopped over onto the path, pausing to hurriedly spoon back as much as she could from the gritty track. She made it to the bottom gates before the gate man could get there. She proudly presented her gritty stew for tea and Dad said, 'That was lovely, duck.'

He never did discover he had eaten a little of the cemetery path, and the coalhouse episode was conveniently forgotten.

I would pass her in the morning coming down the stairs when I was dressed and off to school and she would be going up.

'Where are you going?' I would hiss at her.

'Back to bed. I'm sick,' she'd reply.

'Sick of school - that's all!' I'd say.

'I might be better in a bit...' she answered with a cheeky grin, as she sauntered into her room. When I complained to Mam all I would get was 'You leave her alone!'

However, it wasn't my sister who bought the law to our door. I had been off school for some time as I had not been very well, when one morning there was a knock at the door. This morning, unfortunately, dad was at home. He answered the door to be confronted by a well-dressed man with a folder

The truant found out

under his arm.

'Mr Holmes?' he said.
'Yes,' said Dad.
'I'm the School Attendance Officer and I've been sent to see why your daughter is not, and has not been, in school for some time.'

'What?' Dad said. 'Cynthia is there right now. You've got the wrong Holmes.'

'No, Mr Holmes, it's Betty I have come to see you about. She has had quite some time off lately and you could be liable for prosecution.'

Now, our dad was a very mild-mannered man, and he'd go out of his way to avoid contact with any kind of official, but he reacted angrily at this statement and the threat of prosecution.

'You what?!' he shouted. Mam and I were in the room behind him, wondering what on earth was going on.

'How dare you come here threatening me with prosecution. Do you know how old she is?' The attendance officer was backing away, as he perused his folder. 'She is in the sixth form studying for her A-levels', Dad shouted. 'She could have left school and been at work two years ago if she had wished.' At this point, the man disappeared through the gate, apologising profusely.
But the damage was done. Dad grabbed his coat and said he was going up to Hallcroft, there and then, to give the headmistress what for. 'I'll give them prosecution!' he yelled.

Now it was my turn to panic, begging and pleading with him not to go, saying that I'd never return if he did. But he stormed off. I'd never seen him in such a rage. Then it was Mam's turn. She turned the waterworks on, yelling 'Now look what you've done, he's going to get into trouble. Oh God - the shame!' she wailed. 'Bringing the police to the door.'
'Mam, he wasn't the police,' I retaliated. 'He's the school bobby and if Dad goes into school I'm never, ever going back.' 'School bobby, police - all the same thing. We've never had trouble at this house and now this. Why can't you be more like your sister? We never have any trouble with her.'

I probably didn't want to be like my sister because I didn't want to spend my days sitting in the dark, coal dust in my lungs and all over my uniform. Who knows how many hours she had spent in that coal house? Her saying 'I only did it once' never rang true but I said nothing.

Dad returned, still very angry, saying that the school secretary had told him the Head was unavailable at that time. It was as if a stick had been poked into a wasps' nest in our living room. Everyone was at each other's throats.

A short note was sent to the house in the afternoon from Miss Severn, apologising to Dad that neither herself, as the Deputy Head, or the Head had been available when he called, and she invited him to take tea with them at her house at 3.00pm on Sunday afternoon. He told the girl who had brought the note to go back and tell them he would be there.

Now it was my turn to start shouting. I had a job as a Saturday girl at M&S on Bath Street and I loved it. The manager had said I might have a good career in retail should I decide to go down that route. I glared at dad, shouting 'If you go for tea with them, I'm never going back. I will go to Marks', and they will give me a job.' I had worked for Mackenzie's fruit and vegetable shop at the top of King Street since primary school, first running errands for them. As soon as they realised, I could reckon up a bill quickly and weigh things accurately, they had me behind the counter serving as often as they could get me. I got a Saturday job at Marks' as soon as I was old enough. So going out into the workplace instead of continued study held no fears for me.

My sister, who was setting the table for tea, didn't help the situation. In fact, she was positively revelling in the situation, wandering about, shaking her head and clucking her tongue. She never knew how close she came to losing her pretty little head that day!

Dad, for once, would not be swayed. His dander was well and truly up.

'Don't you worry my girl. I can stick my little finger up in the air when I'm drinking my tea with the best of them!'

It's quite miraculous I didn't have a complete nervous breakdown over it at this point.

So off he went to his afternoon tea, much to my complete disbelief (he was just not the type of man to vent his anger and argue with officials to confront these two very astute and formidable ladies, leaving my mother and I at home in a state of nervous exhaustion over the whole affair.

We needn't have worried. Dad returned gushing, 'What lovely ladies!'

The only little fingers lifted in the air that afternoon had been theirs and Dad had been twisted helplessly around them.

When he started talking, he sounded like the Minister of Education. 'It's so important you take your exams and finish your education, Betty', he parroted. 'You are back in school as of Monday morning and you have some catching up to do.'

So that was it. As always, I took the path of least resistance and returned. I eventually left school and went to art college. I had been teaching for some years before giving up my post, as I wanted to bring up my new baby. However when I saw a part-time post advertised at Hallcroft, I applied, thinking that I could have the best of both worlds. I was sent an appointment for interview but after a little thought I decided it wouldn't be practical and withdrew my application.

A week or so later there was a knock at the door. I answered it and, to my amazement, there stood Miss Severn who I hadn't seen since leaving school about ten years previously. I invited her in and she came straight to the point, as she always did, 'What's going on, Betty?' she said 'arrangements have been made for people to attend for interview and now you throw a spanner in the works!' I explained that it wasn't really practical to get the baby from Awsworth to my mother to care for in Ilkeston and then walk to Hallcroft early in the morning. She wasn't impressed with my excuse, saying the least I could do was to attend the interview. I gave in (as usual) and agreed. I later sat waiting with three other applicants feeling like a timewaster and fraud but was offered the post and accepted. I never regretted changing my mind. It was like going home.

I had always suspected that Miss Severn might have had a hand in that visit from the attendance officer and her seeking me out years later to give me that gentle dressing down pretty much proved it in my mind. Her way perhaps of giving me a kick up the backside (again).

I once broached the subject years later when I had returned to teach at Hallcroft. We were having a cup of tea in the staff room together. She smiled and said, 'Oh, I remember your dad, Betty. A lovely man and so amenable.' She never really answered my question.

Miss Severn was a brilliant teacher and deputy head who, I think, would have become the headmistress if the boys' and girls' parts of Hallcroft hadn't merged. She was a very caring teacher who had set her sights on my career path, and it was wonderful in later years to work with her and have her become a good friend.

CHAPTER 24

Shortwood, Cossall a.k.a. Bluebell Wood 1950s

Sundays up to and through the fifties, were very different from nowadays. Everything closed, towns were silent and deserted buses ran hourly services (that's not changed); even pubs closed earlier, but we knew no different.

Many kids were packed off to Sunday School or church, so the usual noise of the baby boomers playing and making a din in the streets was often absent or subdued, a little at least.

Our dad, like many miners, loved nature and he would often take my younger sister and I walking in the countryside in the spring and summer and we knew the names of all the wildflowers and different birds from a very early age.

'Come on,' he'd say when we came home from Sunday School, 'we'll go up to Bluebell Wood and pick a few bluebells for your mam and mama before dinner.'

My sister would be rolling her eyes at the thought of the distance we'd have to walk. 'Or', he would say, 'you can get off up to Grandma's for a bath.'

No contest.

He used to work at a pit called Oakwood Grange that was up near Shortwood or as everyone local called it, Bluebell Wood. 'Stop moaning" he'd say, "I had to do this walk twice a day and then work up to my waist in water sometimes. It was a wet pit.

Along the bottom cut, up to the swing bridge and crossing the top cut we would go. Up Pig Todd Lane, through Cossall to where the road bends, then we would follow the path up to Shortwood: a beautiful old wood hundreds of years old with the ground so thickly carpeted with English bluebells it was impossible to stray from a path without crushing them. An unbelievable sight, not seen anywhere today.

We were only allowed to pick very small bunches, and dad would get very angry when he saw children, sometimes even with their parents, who should have known better, coming away with great arms full. These would be dead of course within a day even if put in water.

So, you can imagine his anger when the outcroppers moved in and bulldozed that beautiful wood for the coal that was beneath it.

The coal was soon gone, and the ancient wood could never be replaced. Now we learn, all these years later, that they haven't forgotten us, and they are coming back to tear up all the land on Robinettes on the other side of the road.

Small consolation I know, but at least there are no more woods for them to destroy.

No More Walks In the Wood

Walk in the woods
We and the trees and the way
Back from the fields of play
Lasted as long as we could
No more walks in the wood

John Hollander 1929 - 2013

CHAPTER 25

The Ilkeston Inter-Schools Sports Day

As Ilkeston's children begin the summer holidays, I remember one of the final events we looked forward to with eager anticipation before the summer break. The Inter-Schools Sports Day marked the end of school and the beginning of our holiday.

This school sporting spectacular was always an exciting occasion. All the schools in Ilkeston would bring along their athletically blessed pupils and we would look forward to them competing against the best of the other schools. We would make our way to the recreation ground in the afternoon where we would all sit in tiers alongside the track, just as it remains today.

All the schools were kept separate, but alongside each other, and there was terrific rivalry! The noise as each of the track events were run was deafening, with children shouting and cheering, teachers trying to keep order and kids

Inter Schools Sports Day, Ilkeston Rec.

being threatened with dire consequences if they didn't behave! Having said that, there was never any disruptive behaviour that I can recall. Behaving in a way that would bring your school into disrepute would not have been tolerated at all, apart from, that is, the friendly and expected cat calling between the 'Bennerley Bucket Bangers' and the 'Roman Candles', and of course the 'Gladdo Boys'; and perhaps a little sniggering from all of them about the red tassels the Grammar school prefects wore on their school caps!

The boys of that era will remember, before pupils started taking their own sports kit to school, how children would all delve into a big cardboard box and find a pair of shorts to fit for PT and put them back when the lesson finished for the next class. I shudder to think how often they were washed or, should I say, not washed, from one term to the next - hygiene not being deemed quite so important then, I think.

The Cavendish School was an all girls school that my sister attended. She would walk from Blake Street to Cavendish Road School each morning and walk back home for her lunch at 12.00pm, with just enough time to eat lunch, before walking (or often running if Mam hadn't got your dinner ready to put on the table when you got in) back again for the afternoon period, and then walk home at 4.00pm. I did the same from Hallcroft as this was considered quite normal in those days.

The Grammar and Hallcroft schools were single sex schools with two separate Head Teachers; Gladstone was all boys and Bennerley and the Catholic schools seemed to be quite happy in their mixed classes.

As all the schools gathered together it was an inevitability that the sound system would often start 'playing up' during the races and the teacher, who was commentating, would finish up tapping a dead mic with his finger and looking helpless. Children constantly dashed from their groups alongside the track to the queue patiently waiting their turn to drink from the water fountain. Is it still there, I wonder?

The Mayor would present cups to the proud schools and, often, the winners of the Ilkeston Inter-Schools Sports would go on to be entered in the Derbyshire Inter-School Cross Country Races and Track Events. This was a different kettle of fish altogether with some superb runners competing from across the county's schools. I have no idea when all these things ceased – maybe when all the schools started to amalgamate.

The better class of school (or so we thought when the eleven-plus was given such prestige, for right or for wrong) like the Grammar or Hallcroft school, wore uniforms and tended to behave with a little more decorum than some of the other schools. However, when it was all over and you all went home - many probably to the same street and often the same house as siblings who went to different schools - we all rubbed along quite happily together and the rivalry ceased.

CHAPTER 26

Teddy Boys

Hickinbottom's Tailors of Ilkeston was a very good tailor's shop that made bespoke suits for men; the shop's reputation for quality suits and clothes was widespread.

When young men started wearing Edwardian style, long, brightly coloured coats or black drape coats and tight trousers, Hickinbottom's was the place to go if you could afford it.

Situated on the corner of Heanor Road and Granby Street where Hamilton's Schoolwear is now, youths and young men would come from as far as Nottingham and Derby to be fitted.

The suits or coats would take four or five weeks to be finally finished, with a couple of fittings in between. He would charge thirty to forty pounds for a fitted suit in the fifties, which was a lot of money when many people were

Hickinbottoms Heanor Road/Granby Street. Circa 1954

only earning about ten pounds a week.

They were called Teddy boys and gave everyone a good laugh in their long, brightly coloured coats, tight trousers and thick-soled shoes that were called brothel-creepers.

The lads thought they looked the bee's knees and certainly brightened the place up but could look very menacing too. There were many fights, especially outside the Premier Dance Hall on the corner of Market Street and White Lion Square, where many of Ilkeston's teenagers gathered on a Saturday night for the weekly dance.

CHAPTER 27

Bonfire Night on 'Johnny's' in the 1950s

The fifth of November, or Bonfire Night, was a completely different affair from today's celebrations. Precautions were non-existent and streets often had their own bonfire night with fires actually in the street. There were no cars then and fires were often lit only yards away from the terraced houses.

I personally never saw bonfires in streets; we were lucky - we had Johnny's playing field or Wash Meadow, as it is officially named now, which was located at the bottom of Blake Street where I lived so I never went anywhere else.

Most families had their own celebration in their backyard. Family and friends would get together and let off a few pretty fireworks and if they had a garden, they enjoyed a bonfire.

There were no official celebrations, unlike today, but Guy Fawkes Night was a really big deal to forties and fifties children. In the run-up to the big night the kids involved in the bonfire, (ours was a large one on Johnny's, so there were lots!) would be out scavenging bits of wood and rubbish. Neighbours would often take the opportunity to get rid of their old furniture. It would all be dragged to the fire and stacked up until it became a mountain, and finally the guy would be sat on top.

Children would be busy making guys, usually a pair of trousers, a shirt, a mask and a coat stuffed with paper. It would then be placed on a trolley or old pram and towed to a good site where plenty of people passed. A big notice would be placed around the guy's neck saying 'SPARE A PENNY FOR THE GUY.' In some cases, a smaller sibling would be sat on the trolley with a large coat and a mask on with the notice around his neck, until, he would get fed up and go home in tears.

Bonfire Night at Home © 1950

People were surprisingly generous, many recalling their own younger days, perhaps, and would throw a copper or two into the collection box and the money would usually be spent on fireworks. Boys would often fill their pockets with penny bangers called 'Little Demons' and 'Atom Bombs'. They would then throw them at each other like grenades. They made terrific bangs when they exploded. An even better 'sport' was to throw one of these or a 'Jumping Jack' into a crowd of girls, causing much squealing and stampeding in all directions. Strange as it may seem, with such shenanigans going on, I don't recall anyone getting hurt. Thankfully, we are careful about making children aware of the firework code now.

'Bonfire raids' were commonplace. A big fire would be prepared on the nearby Potters playing field or Ashes as it was called. There was also another big one at The Junction. All the children from each area would raid any fires they could to enhance their own. So, bonfires were guarded as well as they could be. Attending school meant that many were left unguarded throughout the day but truants (who obviously thought it well worth the risk of the cane the next day if returning without a note from their parents) would take advantage of the lack of guards and pillage other gangs' fires. Really bad boys would also delight in setting fire to a completed fire and some bigger boys apparently stayed with them all night although I never knew anyone who was allowed to do so.

Even when the weather was not so good or it was raining on the night, the bonfire would somehow manage to be lit. The streets hung with smoke the following day, especially with all the coal fires helping to clog the atmosphere.

Every bonfire night our family had to go through the same ritual, even though there was a giant fire all ready for lighting a couple of hundred yards away. We would stand in our little yard whilst dad would prepare the display. He bought the same fireworks every year: one packet of sparklers, two Volcanoes and the star of the show, a large Catherine Wheel.

With a big lump hammer in one hand and firework in the other, the pin would be tapped gently through the firework into the coalhouse door, often resulting in a black fingernail or bent pin. The fuse would be lit, and everyone held their breath because it never went the way it was supposed to. The Catherine Wheel would smolder, splutter, turn slowly a couple of times and fly off at high speed scattering us all. Dad would curse and Mam and Mama would laugh and say, 'Gordon you're useless!' And that would be the end of the display... well, it was after the last sparkler was waved around (Dad didn't believe in spending a lot on fireworks!) and we were finally free to go to the proper bonfire on Johnny's.

Halloween seems to have taken over as the biggest autumnal celebration in the country now. Even though we still celebrate the fifth of November, it is nothing compared to the excitement the children felt as they prepared their own in the run-up years ago. However, common sense (and health and safety) mean that such times are consigned to history!

CHAPTER 28

The Carol Singers

Our generation were much the same as today's children when Christmas started to loom on the calendar; we were all wishing for a white Christmas and sack loads of presents!

As soon as it clicked into December we would be out carol singing often to the cries of someone from inside the targeted house shouting, 'Come back nearer Christmas!' or perhaps it would be, 'not tonight, thank you!' Often, the younger ones (who thought they could get away with it would hurry their way through one verse of some carol or other with a gabbled finale of, 'Christmas is coming, the goose is getting fat, please put a penny in the old man's hat. If you haven't got a penny, a ha'penny will do. If you haven't got a ha'penny, well, God bless you!' This was followed by a sharp 'rat-a-tat-tat' on the door. The door would open and a miner, perhaps still in his muck, would appear.

'Yes?'

'We are carol singing, mister,' one might reply.

'Oh! Go on then,' the miner would say.

'But we've already done it!'

'Well, I never heard anything - do it again!'

The group's one verse was grudgingly sung again in front of their audience of one, not helped with someone inside shouting, 'Shut that door, you're letting the cold in!'

The man would go on to say, 'Well, that's not worth much - you need to learn more carols!'

'How much has the miserable old devil given us?' would be asked as soon as the door was shut firmly behind him.

The streets around us were very territorial and there were lots of kids of various ages playing out until quite late in the evening in all the streets off Station Road. You would be singing away, putting on a good performance, having learned lots of carols or with the words written down and a torch to read by, hoping to make a good impression in neighbouring streets. Suddenly, a snowball would come whizzing past your ear and explode on one of the other singers' heads. When the bombardment got too hot we would make a run for it back to Blake Street, where snow barricades had been already prepared on each corner of the street for such eventualities!

Piles of snowballs were already neatly stacked and ready to repel any pursuant.

The bravest were the boys with angelic voices – they knew it too! They wanted to make as much money as possible from their musical gift and share it with no-one. They would bravely set out, alone, around the neighbourhood singing their hearts out. You would frequently see them returning with lots of pennies but sometimes at a run, plastered with snowballs!

In snowy or icy conditions, the first job for us kids was to make the best slide possible – be it at school, in the playground or in the local streets. Growing lines of children would wait their turn to go down the sheet of ice, arms 'windmilling' to keep their balance, at high speed.

Today's children (not being used to such boisterous antics and regular snowfall, would perhaps spend more time on their bottoms than on their feet if they tried to copy the distances we slid! It was all very good-natured most of the time, apart from one or two of the boys who sometimes ended up disputing who was 'cock of the neighbourhood' at school and would occasionally have a bit of a set-to. Mostly though, we all went in, cold and wet but happy and sometimes, on a good night, with a few bob to share between us. Christmas was coming...

CHAPTER 29

Christmas Eve

Christmas was an exciting time for both adults as well as children in the forties and fifties. The run up to Christmas began at the beginning of December, not the end of September like today. Shops would begin dressing their windows, even small ones, and the big stores were especially creative and festive.

Most people travelled to and from work and into town by public transport and the double-decker buses would be full downstairs with kids going to school, women and girls going to work in the factories, chattering with friends and neighbours about the coming holiday.

Parties to be planned, fuddles in factories to be arranged and kids excited about forthcoming school parties and the trimming of their classrooms with paper chains and decorations they were making; the excitement grew as the big day got closer.

B.O'Neill 2007

Most men sat on the top deck in a fug of cigarette smoke - they just left it to the women.

'Workmen upstairs, please' the notice said at the bottom of the stairs.

Kids would be practising their carols ready to go carol singing around the neighbourhood and if you could sing a couple of carols with two verses you sometimes got a shilling but usually only a few coppers; good singers could make quite a few bob.

The lazy kids would sing one verse of one carol ending with, 'We wish you a merry Christmas, we wish you a merry Christmas and a happy new year. If you haven't got a penny, a ha'penny will do if you haven't got a ha'penny, well, God bless you'. These kids generally got short shrift from neighbourhoods who were a little overwhelmed with singers.

Our gang usually went up town some evenings to look at the Christmas tree and lights. The tree was especially sent over from Norway and would sometimes look a little tired. However, when I got home and lay thinking about it in my bed, my imagination had improved it dramatically to something more like my painting; much more satisfactory for me!

CHAPTER 30

The Pictures

When I was young I was addicted to The Pictures (cinema). We were lucky in Ilkeston because we had four 'Picture Houses'; The Kings on Bath Street, situated where the entrance to the Albion Centre is now, the Scala (still with us), the Ritz at the end of Coronation Street and the New Theatre at the bottom of Lord Haddon Road, where a nursing home now stands.

If the film had a U certificate, minors were allowed in but if it had an A certificate, you had to be accompanied by an adult. You had to be eighteen to get into X-rated films.

When an A film was being shown (today's PG certificate) it was quite normal to see kids standing outside the picture house in pairs or perhaps the braver ones, alone, waiting for a likely looking couple or older person to

approach the theatre. I was always one of those who liked to go alone. I didn't want the film to be spoiled by a friend constantly whispering to me. I was always engrossed by the storyline, whatever it was, and I would be completely absorbed by whatever was being shown.

If you wanted an adult to get you in you would step alongside your approaching victim, who was often trying to look elsewhere to avoid catching your eye. You had to be firm and to appear confident and you would say loudly "Can you get us in please" offering the couple the money to buy the ticket. Sometimes it would be a brusque "No" but often the couple would have been doing the same as you, only a few years earlier. When I was young, I was pretty naïve, but not naïve enough to approach anyone other than couples. Once inside the theatre, I would do exactly what was expected of me by my newly adopted guardians, and that was to disappear and sit anywhere but with them. This practice went on all across the country; everyone including the picture house staff were aware of this way of getting round the law. Now and again the reel would break during the main feature, accompanied by a groan from the audience.

At the end of the second house the National Anthem would be played, and most people stood still, although there was often a bit of a rush by some, trying to get out before it played.

I have, more than once sat, through the first and second house by going to the toilet when the first house finished and emerging when the second house started, sliding down in the seat trying to avoid the usherette shining their torch on you and asking loudly if you had already watched the film. Some people would come in halfway through the film so would sit into the second house to the part they had come in on. If you could move to a seat near these people you would look as if you belonged.

Sometimes, walking home at just after ten pm, I'd meet Dad coming to look for me, him knowing what I'd been up to, and then home to face an irate mother.

Even though I would go to almost any lengths to feed my addiction to The Pictures -from running errands for neighbours for a copper or two, or collecting any refundable bottles I could find - I would never have dreamed of doing what my husband, Michael, did when the film 'The Body Snatchers' came to Ilkeston.

Reports in the newspapers said that it was so horrifying that people had collapsed with fright, or some would have to leave the theatre, too overcome to sit through the film.

So desperate was he to see this X-rated horror film, he put on his dad's long fawn mac, his trilby hat tilted over his eyes and his dad's pipe, held nonchalantly in one hand whilst offering the money for a one and sixpenny ticket, or whatever the price was then, to the lady in the kiosk. He must have looked a right…! Well, let's just say he looked ridiculous, shall we? He was fifteen and very skinny.

The lady in the kiosk looked steadily at him, and, after a pause, said 'You aren't eighteen, are you?' He was so used to having to tell the truth or face the consequences, he said, 'No.' The lady never said anything, just sat there looking at him, until he picked up his money, turned and walked away down the steps. Even more embarrassing, the lady in the kiosk lived on his aunt's road and knew him anyway. He still blushes when remembering it. He never did see the film, even though it has been on TV since.

Mr Dresser was the best-known cinema manager in Ilkeston. He looked to be seven feet tall, and all the boys would say, 'He was a guardsman during the war.' The tanner rush on a Saturday could be a pretty wild place at the Ritz. You would queue down South Street to get in and when it had filled up, some of the kids would start throwing orange peel, pulling plaits, launching paper planes and, before long, mayhem reigned.

Mr Dresser would come marching down the aisle and bellow that the film wasn't starting until they settled down and that he would be throwing out troublemakers. Peace reigned and he'd march back up the aisle but missiles would start flying again until the lights went down to loud cheers. You were always left on the edge of your seat with the cliffhanger, having to wait until the following week to find out if the hero would get out of his crashed burning car or whatever predicament he had gotten in to. Superman (I think, played by George Reeves) was always landing on window ledges of skyscrapers, but you never actually saw him flying.

When the big picture finished, you would make your way home. Lads would be galloping past you, slapping their own backsides, making clicking noises to make the pretend horse they were riding, that Roy Rogers or Gene Autry had been riding earlier, go faster. Other kids were racing to get to the bus stop on the market to catch the trolley bus coming up South Street, going to Cotmanhay.

These were the golden times of the picture houses. Queues would line up regularly outside cinemas, waiting to go in to see a film. Little did they imagine that by the end of the fifties, many people would own a monochrome TV. The last long queue that I remember outside an Ilkeston picture house, was for the film 'Saturday Night and Sunday Morning' in 1960. I didn't need to be standing outside asking to be sneaked in, by then. Like many, a little later, I lost my fascination for The Pictures.

Funnily enough, the film 'Saturday Night and Sunday Morning' has been shown a couple of times just recently on a couple of TV channels. It was a brilliant film, and it was described by the critics as 'gritty realism'.

However, I thought that Albert Finney, who was excellent as Arthur Seaton, never got the local accent right, whereas Norman Rossington and Hilda Baker, being northerners, found it much easier.

CHAPTER 31

The Gossips

In every street, in most neighbourhoods in the country, not just in Ilkeston, there were 'the gossips'! All the women who lived on a street would be out every morning, rub stoning their windowsills and doorsteps. This practice happened across the country I think, but most definitely in the Midlands and the North. Can you imagine people doing that nowadays?!

In the forties and fifties, to have a dirty doorstep was to be a virtual social outcast! In our house, if you weren't at school, you had to 'step lively and get gone' or you would be sent out with your rub stone, bucket and floor cloth, and a "make sure you do them properly."

The same women would gather every morning when they had finished their doorstep cleaning to share any snippets of information they had picked up.

Often, if the weather was fine but even if it was cold, you could be sent up town on some errand or other and they would still be there when you returned.

Characters and reputations would be slandered by these women - often bitter from suffering a hard life from childhood. How they found time to do all that gossiping, I don't know. In our house, and most houses then, housewives had no gadgets to help with chores and their week was pretty full-on.

Monday would be washday, Tuesday was doing all the ironing as well as the daily cleaning and there was a big Friday cleaning ritual. All the rugs were taken out, shaken and beaten. We also had a baking day, that took nearly all day for our big family which happened on a Thursday. No wonder they looked old before their time!

Summer evenings would see a couple of women out on the street gossiping, soon to be joined by two or three others. They would watch young folk coming down the street - perhaps to the Co-op weekly dance or the Premier Dance Hall on Market Street - dressed in their flared skirts, high heels, bright lipstick and hair done up. They would often walk past the group of women with an exaggerated wriggling of their hips. The women's heads would go down in a huddle, often one of them would shout after the girls, especially if a girl had looked over her shoulder grinning cheekily at them (as they often did to wind the women up!)

'Wot yo' lookin' at?'

'We not talking about yo'!' (even though they were) went the exchange... Often these young women were more than capable of standing up for themselves and gave as good as they got!

The gossips would know everything about everybody in the neighbourhood and were quite capable of making something up or embellishing some small thing. You crossed them at your peril. Even being polite and non-committal could get you labelled as 'stuck up and above yourself.'

When TVs began to become more widespread, after the Queen's coronation, these people spent more time indoors but still managed to miss nothing that happened in the street!

There was one nice, perfectly ordinary lady in our neighbourhood who, on a more lively than usual Saturday night in the Carlton Club, stood on a table and did a little song and dance accompanied by the piano.

It was a one-off, probably on one too many gins. It was all around the neighbourhood by the next day and from that day until she died an old lady, she was spoken of whenever she passed or talked about as the woman who used to dance on the tables in the Carlton, showing her drawers to the club members…

The gossips could be very cruel, and I bet they would have loved Eastenders! Perhaps they would be lost in today's busy society though. For many neighbourhoods, it's a bygone age and now (sadly) many people cannot name more than half a dozen people in their street, despite having lived there for years.

The Gossips

CHAPTER 32

Two Way Family Favourites

Sunday dinner was always special at our house in the fifties, and in most homes across the UK; we were all out of the same mould then, I think. Pretty much everything was closed on Sundays, no shops open, only some on street corners, often illegally.

All the streets and roads were deserted. Buses would only run once an hour and factories were closed. Many people found Sundays pretty grim, especially if it was raining, but it was the norm then and no-one knew any different.

There was general rejoicing when the government relaxed restrictions on Sunday trading although there would have been many long faces if it had been known that change wouldn't come until 1994.

It was the one day of the week that families could get together around the table at lunchtime. Dinner was cooked, put on the table and you all ate together; there were no fast-food outlets then. Everyone was still home at that time and two of Mama's sons, my uncles, were still living with us. We were never short of food. Mama was always baking bread, bottling and preserving. She was a fantastic cook, her and Mam never seemed to stop working and there was a day for every task to be done. They carried on doing what they had done all their lives, even when things were much easier and there was no need for them to work so hard.

Dad always sharpened the carving knife on the doorstep and, over the years, a deep groove had been worn into the step. He would then carve the meat. Our little dog Dinky would be sitting outside the back door hoping for some scraps.

The radio, or wireless as it was called then, would be on and the most popular show of the week would begin, its introduction familiar to everyone. The announcer would say, 'The time in Britain is twelve noon. In Germany it's one o'clock, but home and away it's time for Two Way Family Favourites.' The theme tune known to everyone, 'There's a Song in my Heart' would then begin playing, and I dare bet many of those reading this who were around then can still hum it now.

The programme was hosted by Jean Metcalf and Cliff Michelmore: one broadcasting from Germany and the other from London. They later met and married.

No noisy jazz music was allowed to be played, no banter between the hosts and definitely no mention of fiancées or girlfriends. By decree of the BBC, they wanted to raise the tone and content of the show. Britain was a very narrow society in those days. I do remember it relaxed more later, the BBC that is, not society in general for some time.

The show put families in touch with loved ones serving in the forces and most of the country listened in. We had a large army then, and they were serving all over the world. National Service was in force and young men from the age of 18 would be called up to do two years' service.

Sharpening the carving knife for Sunday lunch

They made up about half of the army and hundreds were killed fighting insurgents abroad in British territories. There were no mobiles then and very few families had a house phone. If you phoned anyone or received a call it was by prior arrangement, to a telephone box in our case at the bottom of Alvenor Street. The show gave a lot of comfort, passing messages to loved ones. Contact would sometimes be made with other far-flung countries where the lads and girls were serving and for that day it would become three-way family favourites.

Service personnel were referred to as BFPO, this meant British Forces Posted Overseas or BAOR, British Army of the Rhine, meaning soldiers serving in Germany. Many families had sons serving in some branch of the forces. National Service finally finished around 1960 and some lads hated it, some loved it. Some got the opportunity to travel to places they would never have seen and others never moved from Catterick or Aldershot.

Speak to any of them now though and they all get nostalgic about their service and old friends, friends lost forever when they were discharged. After dinner was finished, the pots were washed, and Dad always did the washing up and I usually dried. When he held out the tea towel for me to dry this particular day, for some reason I said, 'No I'm not.'

'What? You What?' he yelled, frightening me! This from a man who never raised his voice to us. His face turned red, his eyes stuck out - he had lost it!

I panicked, turned and ran out of the door through the gate down the steps onto Blake Street with him hot on my heels with the tea towel being flailed, 'I'm NOT! I'm NOT!' he was yelling. I knew if he caught me I was going to get my first good hiding. Okay, it would have only been with a dry tea towel but he would have been mortified later.

So, I saved him from himself. I was at the bottom of Blake Street, skidding round the corner at high speed when he was only halfway down, shaking his tea towel in anger. It was the only time in my life I saw my dad lose his temper and the only time in mine I defied him. When I crept in an hour or

so later the family had settled down for the rest of the afternoon,
the pots all washed, dried and put away.

Dad was in his chair behind the News of The World and acknowledged my
return by giving it a shake and a grunt, Mama rolled her eyes and smiled.
Mam jerked her thumb toward the front room and said, 'Piano practice,
now.' I went, for once, without a peep. The paper would be read and there
would be much tutting and sighs coming from behind it. Short comments
and knowing glances exchanged about some articles. You weren't allowed to
read the paper, though, but your interest was piqued by all these supposedly
hidden asides.

As a youngster you would try to make sense of all this by sitting on the lav
and reading the paper the next day. Pretty difficult when it had been cut into
squares and was all mixed up, the relevant newsprint perhaps transferred to
where you couldn't possibly read it. You could come out completely
confused.

Billy Cotton would be shouting 'Wakey, wakey' for his radio show which
was followed by Peter Brough and Archie Andrews, a ventriloquist and his
wooden dummy, and we would listen and laugh. He must have had the gift
of the gab to have got that job. A ventriloquist on the radio! Well, no-one
ever saw his lips move. After that everyone started snoozing and kids would
disappear onto the streets if it was fine and, in my case, I'd finish torturing
the piano.

CHAPTER 33

Wash Meadow Allotments

Alongside Wash Meadow (Johnny's) were allotments that were very well kept and produced a lot of much needed food during and after the war People still grow produce on allotments but nowhere near on the scale they used to and many of these allotments have now disappeared, the land sold to developers.

It is hard for people to imagine today just how busy Wash Meadow used to be. It was often thronged with people: children playing, gardeners tending their allotments and people cutting through from Slack Lane that ran from the end of Wentworth Street.

Beyond the allotments ran the spur line from the main railway line to the Midland Railway terminus at the Town Station, which was at the bottom of

Bath Street, Ilkeston's main high street through the centre of the town. The Tesco superstore now stands on that spot.

Many people would ride the spur for about a penny from The Junction to the Town station.

Ilkeston had three stations at one time, all well used. Beyond the railway line was the large gasometer which rose and fell depending on the amount of gas it held. The gasometer provided all the gas for Ilkeston town. This was before North Sea gas was discovered. Below the gasometer was Cookie's scrap yard.

All this land has now been taken for the Millership relief road.

CHAPTER 34

The Cellar

Our house had a large cellar which had two rooms. One room was filled with coal tipped in through a grate in the street, and the other, which was always very cold in winter and cool in summer, was used to store food in. This room had a long marble thrall where preserves, meat, and other perishables were kept cool. There were no fridges for most ordinary working-class people then.

Many houses had gas meters that were coin fed. Ours was in the cellar, and if the gas went off you would be sent down with a candle to feed pennies into it. Many houses in the forties and fifties had no electricity and relied on gas for their lighting and cooking.

Feeding the meter was a frightening experience for me and my sister and we would be sent down if our dad or our uncles weren't in. In the daytime if

Feeding the gas meter in the cellar © 1950

the door to the next room where the coal was kept was opened a little daylight would filter in from the grate in the street where the coal was tipped, but if it was in the evening or night it was pitch black down there.

Frogs used to fall into the cellar through the grating in the street and get into the storage room. You went in fear and dread of treading on one and squishing it, or worse, one jumping on your foot. My sister, Cynthia, was always yelling and screaming that either she had trodden on something or a spider had touched her. We hated it but Mam would say, 'Stop being a baby and get off down,' but never went herself.

My dad once went down for a bucket of coal and when he came back and set it down on the hearth, a big green frog sat on top of the coal looking at us.

Mam nearly had a fit and dad had to quickly and gently carry it outside to the garden. It was a good job Mam and Mama weren't in alone. I think they would both have had heart attacks, being afraid of frogs, and it would have been no good relying on either my sister or myself to pick one up. We would have definitely dug our heels in and refused. Froggy was a lucky fellow too. He avoided being shovelled into the fire in our dimly lit kitchen later in the evening by a whisker.

A friend of ours, who was in the building trade, told us that a lot of the cellars just above and below Blake Street where we lived had been filled in. Such a shame because those extra rooms, damp-proofed to today's standards, would be a godsend to most people with all the extra belongings we accumulate.

CHAPTER 35

From Guzunder To Down Under: Our Cousin David's Story

Most of the females in our house disliked our cellar, because of what could be lurking down there. Not so much the men, or later mine and my sister's sons who liked nothing better than getting down there when they got the chance and rooting round the bits and bobs left or dumped out of the way.

Our young cousin, David Osborne, who was our uncle Bill's (Boss's son) was once visiting with his Mum and took the opportunity to go down into the cellar exploring. Mama shouted down to him, 'What are you doing down there David? Don't you get covered in coal dust!'

He shouted back, 'I've found a soldier's helmet, Mama.' Peering down the steps she said, 'Is that the Jerry you've got on your head, David? If it gets

stuck it'll have to stay there.'

The cellar had been used by our family as an air raid shelter during the war and it had been kitted out with camp beds, blankets and, of course, a chamber pot commonly called a guzunda, potty, jerry or, in a lot of houses, 'THE BUCKET'. I'm not going to say what my Uncle Ted used to call it, just to get a reaction from Mama (his mam and he'd be told off by Mama whenever he did.)

She'd say, 'You're not too big you know, our Ted.' Even though he'd fought in the war she could still threaten to give him a clout.

In our house Mama always referred to it as 'The Jerry', so named because the shape was like a German soldier's helmet. Bits and pieces remained kicking about in the cellar long after the war was over.

David, completely misunderstanding what she meant, having never used such a thing given he lived in a posh prefab on the Cotmanhay estate, replied, 'No, Mama, it's alright, it's not a German one, it's one of ours.'

David's father, our Uncle (Boss) Bill, my Mum's eldest brother, died when he was only forty one and David was only eleven, leaving his Mum, Kathleen, to bring him up alone. David was blessed with a brilliant memory and recalls his early life being raised in Cotmanhay and being educated at Cotmanhay Infant and Junior School and Bennerley Secondary Modern on Cotmanhay Road. David now recalls his early years living on Skevo Lane (the name given to Skevington Lane by all the kids on the estate.)

David now takes up the story.

My first memories are of having lots of green around me as we backed onto Farmer Bentley's cow field. On two occasions the fence was knocked down by the cows and they would come into our garden, which was my dad's pride and joy, much to his anger. He also had two more allotments where he grew vegetables and flowers, which he then sold. I still have the cutting from the local paper with a picture of myself in a highchair in our new kitchen with Mum. Mum and Dad were one of the first couples to move into the new prefab bungalows on Skevington Lane in 1947. Mum is smiling from ear to ear, beaming at the luxury she now had. The prefab was painted white with the window trims and the doors were painted pea green. We even had a copper to do the washing, a built-in gas fridge with a freezer that was big enough to take a small block of ice cream that we would buy from the Wall's ice cream van that used to come around the new estate.

Ice cream wasn't the only thing delivered to our door. As Farmer George Bentley's farm was only a hundred yards or so away he'd deliver our milk with his horse, Toby, and a cart loaded with milk churns. Mum and other ladies would queue up and hand him their jugs, and he would pour a measure of milk in. When I got a bit older I would follow Mr Bentley and Toby on his rounds with a steel bucket and a dustpan to scoop up any good

stuff Toby left behind for dad's garden. George Henshaw,
who lived on Church Street, also had a horse and cart and had a round on another area of the estate. Mr Henshaw and his horse had their own followers and you wouldn't dare try to trespass on their territory to take their 'good stuff.' His horse once went mad and just bolted, scattering crates and smashing bottles of milk all down Beresford Drive.

Oh, the excitement.

A little further up Church Street, Mr Burton, a local builder also had a milk and egg round that he and his wife did early in the morning before Mr Burton started work. Their son also helped before school and they were lucky enough to make their deliveries in a motor van which he also used in his building work. All hard-working people and with all the new houses, there was plenty of work for all. The Co-op had a big green butchery van where you went up steps that were folded down to allow access. Inside the van was a counter and behind it a little butcher's shop was all rigged up, with fridges and cold cabinets. The butcher was called Ron, if I remember right, and he had a round on the estate and would come once a week; I don't know where else in Ilkeston he would deliver to.

We also had the rag and bone man coming around with his big cart calling, 'We buy old rags, we buy anything - any old rags, old bones or old iron.'

Dad saved bundles of papers and passed them on to him, sometimes he would have goldfish to trade in little bags, and one year mice nested in the bundles of paper (we assumed from the farm) and dad had to burn it all.

Mum reminded me years later how she had been upset in case any of the mice were still inside, especially when we could hear them popping in the flames. Much later the milk was delivered by a 3-wheeler electric van that took over from Bentley's horse drawn milk cart. The milk was in glass bottles. The country was starting to pick itself up after being nearly bankrupt by the war and the bottles had silver or gold foil tops that birds very cleverly used to cut into and drink the cream. Yes, an electric vehicle to deliver milk and to think electric vehicles are deemed new nowadays! We also recycled - all our veggie scraps went into the garden compost with Toby's 'good stuff' and we had a solar and wind powered clothes dryer too. It was a clothes line out in the backyard! It worked a treat, even in winter when the clothes stood frozen stiff and were freeze dried. No one had a dryer then, not on our estate anyway.

Bentley's farm was situated in the fields at the bottom of Skevington Lane and when the haystacks were being taken down, lots of our neighbours would be invited down with their dogs to catch the rats (a lot) that came scurrying out of the hay, with bets being taken among the men as to whose dog would bag the most rats. They were very competitive, and more than a few pints would be sunk in the Bridge Inn or Hand and Heart that night.

We had the same service as the rest of Ilkeston, where our refuse was concerned. Norman's Dust Carts based on Chapel Street collected the rubbish before the Council took it over. The lorries were fitted with sliding covers on each side of the lorry and the dustman would come up the yard, grab the bin and with a lift and a twist would hoist it onto the leather half-moon shoulder pad on his shoulder. He would hurry down to the lorry and tip it in. No mean feat with a lot of the bin being taken up with heavy ashes, often wet from being damped down with water when put in hot from the coal fires we had. A very dirty tough job, done by tough men. They would often just chuck your bin back up the yard to save walking back up and housewives would complain about how roughly they treated their bins.

My dad was the full-time caretaker of Cotmanhay School. Mum was a cleaner there and she would take me to school with her. I would play in the Infants' classroom by myself whilst she worked. I still remember Miss Dawes, the infants' teacher.

I remember, too, the lovely smell that came from the school canteen when they were dishing up, making my mouth water; it smelled absolutely delicious. Later when I was in the Juniors I often got into trouble, although I wasn't a bad kid. I now realise the problem was I couldn't see the blackboard, so they put me at the back of the class, as it was done in those days. I often got the cane from Mr Moon even if whatever had happened wasn't my fault. It didn't do me any harm, I suppose, although it didn't seem to do me much good either, I thought.

Dad was a sergeant major during the war. Gardening and smoking Woodbines, I think, was his way of masking what he had seen and done during the war. Then, at just 41, my dad suddenly died of lung cancer. I was 11 at the time. Mum needed to make ends meet so she became the Grattan's lady for the area as well as being a cleaner at the school. I learned a lot about wrapping up parcels with mum, a skill I still use today. At the age of 13 I worked at Tom Astle's, the butchers, both before and after school, three days a week. I was often late for school in the morning because of work, then late again for the butchers in the afternoon as I had been kept in to do lines in detention - I couldn't win at either end.

I never had any real mates at school as I was a loner. A lad called Tommy Green was just about my best mate. He couldn't see too well but I could see better than he could, so I helped him where I could. I was hopeless at everything at school, though, except science, which I found very interesting.

When, in my last term at Bennerley, I applied for three apprentice positions and, surprisingly, was accepted by all three. An electrician and fitter with the NCB (National Coal Board had the better prospects, I thought, so I accepted the apprenticeship at the pit. I started off at Coppice Colliery and I was down the pit for training. After only 6 months I got sick with jaundice and was off for several weeks. When I returned, they put me in the time office and phone exchange for almost a year while I built up my strength again. Here I stayed until the pit began to close. The manager then got me a job at Stanton Ironworks - they were very good to me. I was now 17 when I met up with my mum's old friend Olive and her daughter, Carol. Carol had been living with her parents in Canada for a few years. We clicked straight away, and I moved to Portsmouth to be near her. Two years later we emigrated to Australia together.

We arrived in Melbourne on January 1st, 1968 - a new start in a new year - something to remember. All industry was closed for a month over Christmas, so I walked the industrial sites and eventually found a cabinet maker open on Jan 3rd. I asked the boss for a job, saying "Anything, part-time, full-time, try me for a week and if I don't suit no need to pay me, a free week for you." I started that day and was full-time by the end of the week. I worked at several jobs over the years which all taught me additional skills. Carol and I split amicably after two years and on New Year's Eve, seven years to the day of arriving in Australia, I had my first date with my now wife Beverley. It was another new year and another new life starting, although I didn't know it then. I first met my wife Beverley when I bought a car on the never-never; she was the beautiful girl behind the counter who would take my car payments, 43 years on and I feel I am still paying that car off!

It used to be just a bit of my wages she took but for the past 42 odd years it has been every penny I ever earned that has changed hands. I was, and still am, a very lucky man having the love of a good woman. I had had several jobs and over the years I picked up a number of different skills. I put this knowledge to good use and a couple of years later I became self-employed, got married, began building our home and started a family all in the same year.

Due to an allergy I had to some timbers that are native to Australia, such as the Western Red Cedar, I started using steel instead of timber to make gates. I was making steel gates that were like big cabinet doors. I was so successful in this line of work I had to start employing others as I had won several contracts. Then my hobby of electronics came into play. Electronic automatic gates now became my forte, the bigger the better.

My wife Beverley had had a bad fall whilst we were visiting the UK in the late seventies. She was initially told by her surgeon in the UK, "My dear, you will probably never walk again." I cannot (or should not) say what she told that surgeon, it was not ladylike, but the surgeon hadn't met an Aussie before. She was determined then and still is that she would walk normally again.

I retired in 2007, mainly due to Beverley's ill health that has plagued her since that accident despite her doggedness and can-do and won't-give-in attitude; she has, only recently, had even more surgery.

That's my life so far, a Bennerley under-achiever, who has progressed through a life with more than a few bumps in the road and more than a few tears along the way. But I have come out the other end a happy guy that is comfortable in retirement mainly due to always being prepared to work hard, do my bit and to the very best of my ability and meeting a good woman who moulded me without me losing my freedom.

I am so pleased that I moved to Australia, it is a great place to get somewhere if you don't mind a bit of hard graft and to put your heart into whatever you do. I retired early mainly due to my wife's physical health, and I too have been a little under the weather for a time lately. We are both now on the mend though and we are determined to enjoy our retirement, and our growing family, at last. We have a little place we visit whenever we can with our grown-up kids and our grandchildren, and we all love it. There is loads for them to do and a cracking golf course.

Betty continues:

David became a successful businessman through hard work, marrying his Australian girl in the early years and building up his business from scratch. With her support, he finishing up trading across Australia, mainly New-South Wales and Victoria, a vast area, even doing work for the High Commission in Fiji and winning contracts with the Australian Army in East Timor. All this whilst raising a family and also later caring for and supporting his wife, Beverley. David doesn't miss working now as he says all the red tape involved in every job was a real bind when he finally sold the business. Beverley is still suffering with her back injuries and one or two more recent problems, but David has never flagged in his care for her and I'm sure they will both win through in time.

David's only regret was in never getting his mum (Kathleen) out to Australia sooner to spend more of the latter part of her life over there with them. However, she did get to Australia and was naturalized before she died and when she died it was with all her family around her.

David says, 'Even though Australia has been my home for most of my life now, my roots will always be in Ilkeston, of course, and I still feel I'm close whenever I sit down and read the local newspapers.'

CHAPTER 36

Monday was Washday

Washday at our house was a day to be dreaded; it was a pleasure to go to school on Monday morning to get out of the way as it was a full day's job. Mam used to pound away with the dolly tub or turn the mangle, Mama would be scrubbing collars.

Most men's shirts were made with no collar; a collar would be attached separately with a small stud that would fix to the back of the shirt, called a collar stud. A man might only own two shirts: one on his back and the other in the wash, but he could have seven clean starched collars to fasten to his shirt, one for each day, if he was well off.

Most workmen would usually only own a couple, to be used when wearing their best clothes. Shirts with collars attached were more expensive to buy and didn't get cheaper until later.

Wash Day.

I would have to fetch my uncle's collars (when he lived with us)
from an old woman at the bottom of the street who used to starch collars to
earn a few shillings. If I brought them back with the slightest speck of soot
or a smudge on them, he would go absolutely spare and throw them across
the room in a temper.

'Don't you shout at her,' Mama would say, 'fetch them yourself if you aren't
satisfied.'

The copper used to have a fire lit under it for boiling clothes and the house
fire would be up the chimney back so it was very hot and steamy, and
tempers would get very frayed.

When you got home from school and if it had been raining, your stomach
would sink when you saw all the washing strung across the kitchen.
In the evenings you would be plonked into the copper, which was still full of
hot water, for a bath. This could be pretty horrible.

The fire had often not long gone out from under the copper, so the bottom
was still hot, and it felt all slimy with all the soap that had settled. You were
hopping about from foot to foot, slipping and sliding all over the place,
complaining loudly. You would often come out with red finger marks on
your leg or bum from a slap.

All the germs on you were dead though.

Boiled alive!

CHAPTER 37

Passing Out Parade

Michael (my husband) and I always watch the Remembrance Sunday ceremony in Whitehall starting before 11.00am on the TV and the parade on the Market Square in Ilkeston. He will go into town and join the crowd while I stay at home to watch.

2021 was very different with lockdown restrictions but, having said that, very well carried out. And, as with most occasions that are marked by the British, we know how to do things properly.

Last year Michael went to the parade on the marketplace and came back full of praise for the CCF (Combined Cadet Force). He commented on the large contingent of cadets present and how smart they all were. He was particularly impressed with the air cadets who were immaculate, shoes highly polished and uniforms so smart. The two young ladies who marched across the square to lay their wreath were so precise in their marching and drill, a pair of regular guardsmen couldn't have bettered. Well done, Ilkeston's youth. There are so many lovely young people who are contributing so much to society, and we need to hear more of their stories.

Ilkeston has, I believe, always had a cadet force post WW2. Initially it was the army cadets alone in Ilkeston and they were called the Derbyshire Yeomanry or 'DYs'. I wasn't aware of them until I went to Hallcroft Girls School. If we had something on in the evening, we would sometimes see them through the classroom windows marching up and down on the girls' top playground with their adult instructors.

Some of them were big lads who looked as if they were not far off being called up, or conscripted, as it was known. This was at a time when most young men had to serve for two years in the army. Others marching were young lads, just old enough to join at age eleven or twelve perhaps. I would sometimes see them on my way home in the evening, running about in pairs on 'Hilly Holies', the green space adjacent to the cemetery, with a map and compass in their hands.

Michael would try to encourage our young grandsons to become cadets when they were old enough. It reminded me of a story of someone close to us, whose son was army mad when young and couldn't wait to get into the cadets.

His mother was dead set against it. She knew her father-in-law had fought throughout the first world war; he had been gassed and wounded and was very lucky to survive. Her husband had spent most of the six years of WW2 away and had been badly burned and scarred. Her brother, too, had been a regular in the Marines and had fought in France and Burma. 'No way is any son of mine having anything to do with the military!' she said.

However, with pressure from her husband and father-in-law, and being told that the discipline would be good for him, she eventually relented and allowed him to join.

He proudly donned his uniform and attended his first weekly meeting, only to be told he looked like a… well, I won't say what!

His father agreed and said, 'you aren't going out looking like that again!'

He instructed him on how to care for his kit. His beret was soaked, fitted around a large dinner plate and put into a hot oven until it had dried and shrunk so that it fitted neatly onto his head. He showed him how to heat the handle of a spoon over a candle and burn all the dimples from the toecaps of his boots and then to rub round and round with spit and polish until they shone like gleaming mirrors. The hapless lad said he couldn't get the hang of it, so his dad would end up showing him again. He became so engrossed in bulling his boots he seemed to revert to his military years. He always finished up doing them for him. His father said he was, in his opinion, 'definite officer material.' He took to having a batman like a duck to water. Well, he had a batman and batwoman too. His ability to iron 'tramlines' into his trousers was exemplary. He couldn't be trusted to do the job so his mother would finish up doing those too! Within just a couple of meetings, he was being complimented on being so well turned out.

'He has no shame,' his father would say.

On Sunday mornings the cadets all used to march down
Gladstone Street and Queen Street to the recreation ground with their rifles
slung over their shoulders. On they would go to the bottom of Derby Road
and on to what was called 'Manor Floods.' They would then play their war
games all morning in the surrounding fields and woods.

They all carried .303 army rifles - obsolete weapons used during WW2.
They were issued with a few blank cartridges each to fire and even had a
light machine gun and thunder flashes. These were, I was told, like giant
banger fireworks which would be thrown by the instructors. It would sound
like a pitched battle as gunshots and explosions echoed around West Hallam
on Sunday mornings. Nowadays I'm pretty sure cadets are not allowed to
wander around the countryside with firearms!

The boy's father told me, 'He went on his first exercise and was over the
moon that he had been issued with a rifle and blanks.' At the end of the
exercise the lad in charge of his section asked if anyone had any blanks left.
They had, so it was decided to put the new boy in front of a firing squad. He
was duly 'shot' and peppered with the paper from the inside of the
cartridges.

His father was very angry when hearing about this, explaining that the paper
came out at quite a high velocity and could cause injury if discharged too
close to someone.

'That's it,' said his wailing mother, 'he's not going again!'

His dad told me he'd seen grown men cry because they had to go in the
army but never anyone crying because they'd got to come out. In the end,
because he kicked up so much fuss, it was decided that his father would go
and have a word with the Captain in charge and was duly assured that such
a thing would never happen again.

The cadet hut in the corner of the Hallcroft Girls' playground was where all
the firearms and equipment were kept and, by all accounts, very well run.
The boys would sometimes be allowed to use the Drill Halls shooting range,
and, occasionally, were even taken to Bisley to live fire on the ranges.

One Remembrance Sunday, the cadets were on parade for the ceremony. It was unusually warm for the time of year and the full array of ceremonial representatives from the police and veterans were there, stood in ranks, around the square and Cenotaph. Ilkeston's Mayor and Mayoress, along with council dignitaries, joined the ranks.

The boy's grandparents had driven from London to see him on parade and were so proud to see him so well turned out (courtesy of batman and batwoman.) Soon their faces changed as they looked on in quiet consternation as he started swaying back and forth until he finally fainted, overcome with the heat. He fell very gracefully into the arms of the adult NCO who had also been watching him. With his hands beneath the lad's armpits, the NCO dragged him through the ranks, his boot heels scraping across the ground and deposited him on to one of the benches in front of the library.

His father and grandfather, after watching in mortification, melted into the crowd but not before taking a photo of their pride and joy being fussed over and fanned by his mother and grandmother and a St. John's Ambulance man wafting smelling salts under his nose. The picture was later put into the family album.

He was never allowed to forget this and whenever his grandparents were over, an earnest discussion would begin across the dinner table between his father and grandfather about the boy's two cousins who were in the Girl Guides and Brownies and 'what a tough bunch they were.' The lad would finish up leaving the table, meal unfinished, in a rage, no mercy shown, from two old soldiers.

The next drama came when he went away to summer camp. They had only been there a day when his best friend was badly injured in an accident that left him with a life changing injury. 'That's definitely it,' said his mother. 'He's finished. I want him out!' His father and grandfather once again intervened on his behalf, telling his mother 'You can't wrap him in cotton wool, he's got to grow up.'

His grandparents had come over again and they all drove down to the camp on the open day and watched as their pride and joy marched up and down, carrying out his rifle drill and ending on a high in the star squad of the week.

She relented again but was not happy and meant to have her way, by hook or by crook. Eventually the poor lad's laziness was his downfall, and the opportunity came gift wrapped to her soon enough with no arguments from anyone.

It was cadet meeting evening, and as usual the young soldier was missing whilst his parents were busy getting his kit ready for the evening's parade. His dad was buffing toecaps and blancoing his belt and puttees. His mother was ironing his shirt and uniform. 'What on earth has he got in his pocket?' she grumbled, hitting an obstruction in his tunic with the iron. Unbuttoning it she reached inside, moaning woefully, 'Oh my God!' 'What?' said his father.

She held up a Rizla cigarette rolling machine, a packet of cigarette papers and a little envelope containing tobacco, along with the remains of 'nud ends' from which it been harvested. 'That is it! He is done! Whatever you say. What are they teaching him there and what's this in here?'
She unbuttoned the other breast pocket and pulled out a neatly folded piece of paper. She unwrapped this and, to her horror, found a page from the magazine 'Health and Efficiency.' Staring back at her were four voluptuous naked ladies vigorously playing tennis. 'Oh! Oh! No! I'll kill him when he comes in!'

His goose was cooked. That was it.

When he finally appeared, it was to find his uniform neatly wrapped in brown paper with his boots perched on top. 'You can take this lot back tonight and tell them you won't be going again.' No amount of begging, promising and protesting that he was 'only looking after the finds for someone' would move her.

'You are done, done, done!' she said. 'What next, cards and dice?!'

How could you go round picking up cigarette ends out of the gutter,' she cried with mortification.

'I didn't,' he said, 'they were only yours and Dad's!'

'I can't help you this time,' his dad said. 'You broke the number one cardinal rule of all soldiers which you should have known. If you are going to do something wrong…. don't get caught!'

A budding military career nipped in the bud…

CHAPTER 38

To Market, to Market: Shopping in Ilkeston in the Fifties

Ilkeston Saturday market used to be very busy. It was the best market in Derbyshire and people would come from miles around to visit.

Saturday was when my sister and I were sent up to get the best bargains. Children were more used to running errands in the fifties. Ours wasn't an errand on a Saturday morning though, it was a big, exciting expedition for us and we loved and looked forward to it!

Convenience shops were noticeable on many street corners and most people would 'bit and bob' throughout the week, alongside weekly trips to the market. They had no choice; money was short, and wages were low for the majority. Very few people had a fridge so food couldn't be stored for long.

The Co-op was the mainstay of our town and for many across the nation. People loved it for the 'Divi' that the Co-op paid out annually and you could

get anything from food, to hardware, to having your house
painted and decorated or going for a meal or function. You could also run
up a bill and pay it off within reason, I think. The threat of losing your 'Divi'
ensured people remained on the straight and narrow and kept up their
repayments. With the Co-op catering for almost every need from birth to
death, it was a national, commercial giant. We could never have imagined it
would practically disappear in the not-too-distant future.

Supermarkets, as we know them now, didn't really come into Ilkeston until
the 1960s and the market was where people bought the bulk of their
produce. We would be sent out on a Saturday morning with our bags, a long
list and strict instructions as to what stall to go to. 'And not that miserable
old devil (or words to that effect) on the corner with second-rate stuff who's
not nice to his wife and kids! And don't squash the cream cakes from
Stacey's on your way back!' As you went through the door your final orders
were shouted after you 'and don't let them palm you off with any old
rubbish and don't forget to get the stewpot from Ward's!' Added to this
were the final words every child in Ilkeston was familiar with, 'Un keep on
corsy!' (the pavement.)

Usually, we were told to make sure we had a clean vest and pants on before
we went out - just in case we were knocked over whilst out. God forbid that
you'd shame your Mam with a dirty vest on if a bus ran over you!)

The market was so crowded, people could only shuffle around very slowly
looking over the shoulder of others being served at the stalls. If someone
stopped to talk to a friend, which everyone was doing all the time, people
moved even more slowly as they passed.

Getting served could be a problem when you were small. Some women had
no qualms about pushing you out of the way to get to the front, but the
stallholders were very good at spotting you. The stalls were all lit with oil or
paraffin lamps hanging from the stall tops, and stall holders would be
competing to see who could shout the loudest!

We just don't hear the sounds of that market anymore. It's difficult to
describe so many people moving around a relatively small area all nattering,

vendors shouting, buses and lorries along with other traffic droning up Bath Street and down South Street or vice versa. There was a constant buzz of sound all day long. Midland General blue and cream double-decker buses packed with people arriving from or going to Cotmanhay, Nottingham, Hallam Fields or as far away as Ripley and Derby - all disgorging more and more people, such was the popularity of our market.

Every Saturday morning a policeman would stand right in the centre of the road on the junction of Wharncliffe Road in front of the Town Hall directing traffic, dressed in his white coat and armbands, changing duty every couple of hours.

How sad to see what our once-famous Saturday market has declined to today…

Ilkeston Saturday Market

CHAPTER 39

A Sleeping Policeman and a Long and Winding Road

My husband has always been a keen cyclist, not, I might add, Tour de France material, but he uses it every day and has done whenever possible since childhood. He always used it to get to wherever he worked, even cycling home from Nottingham when he finished work in the afternoon and cycling back over the footpaths and bridleways through Strelley village and back again the same way after having his meal and a shower to a part-time job he had, driving a Skills coach. Then it was home the same way late at night, across the bridleways in the dark and up again for work at 06.00am. It was a tough time for us.

It's his proud boast that he has never fallen off his bike! All the numerous accidents he has had over the years have been the result of his cycle malfunctioning or his 'favourite', poorly maintained roads. It resulted in the

radiographer at his last accident commenting about the
number of X-rays he'd had over the years. 'Yes', he said, 'I'm a keen cyclist.'
'Mmm,' she replied, 'not a very good one it seems!'

So naturally I used to worry, especially on dark mornings when he would cycle down the bypass to Bulwell on his way to work in Bestwood Village. Even he had to admit hearing large goods vehicles thundering down behind him and passing at high speed, with seemingly only inches to spare, could be a little nerve racking.

One morning I was at work when the Headmistress came to my room looking rather stern and said, 'there's a phone call for you Betty in my office. I'll look after your class.' I knew it was going to be bad news. It was, he had been hit by a van and taken to Queen's Medical Centre in Nottingham.

When I saw him he was battered and bruised with fractured ribs, a broken shoulder and suspected concussion, having been knocked out. They kept him in for a while and he had an operation to put a plate and screws in his shoulder. Our son fetched him home when he was able to be discharged but things didn't go well as he was still in a lot of pain.

Eventually he was sent to the Park Hospital in Burnstump Country Park about twelve miles or so from us on the other side of Papplewick for further surgery on his shoulder. Our son took him and fetched him when he was able to come home. However, I had to take him the following week to see the consultant. He had his arm strapped up in a sling across his chest to his neck, still in pain but suffering quietly (not!)

I must admit I didn't like driving him. Even though he never said anything or criticised I felt I was being judged and I watched him from the corner of my eye for any tells, like wincing, or sharp intakes of breath or the involuntary movement of his hand to cover his eyes.

We made the trip through Watnall, Hucknall and Papplewick, and then in to the Burnstump Country Park where the Park Hospital is situated. It is a twelve mile or so journey. The drive went smoothly, and there was no

advice, complaints or involuntary twitches from the patient.

After seeing the consultant he came out and said, 'I've got to see him again next week.'

'Oh,' I thought, 'more time off work!'

The ride home was good, smooth and steady and then, disaster! Coming down a steep hill, and nearly home lay a sleeping policeman (speed bump) across the road, cunningly disguised, painted in the same colour as the black tarmac it lay on.

It was one of those particularly vicious narrow black rubber ones. The patient gave a warning squawk but too late, we hit it at about 30mph (ok it might have been 40, but it should have been 30!) I thought the car was going to disintegrate. Oh, the dramatics! The groan of pain and despair, with his head resting against his window making little whimpering noises.

I could feel the rage bubbling up inside me, but nothing was said. We got home and I think we both thought it best to have a quiet period. We were still giving each other the silent treatment a week later.

I woke on his appointment morning to find him gone. I couldn't figure out where he was. I knew he hadn't got a lift and there were no bus connections. I got ready, waiting for him to appear but he didn't. Then, after an hour or two, a thought struck me but no, that would have been ridiculous. I went to the shed and found his bike missing!

Oh no, surely not, he couldn't in the state he was in - to cycle all that way with one arm strapped round his neck was impossible. I quickly got ready and drove to the hospital. I went in and there he was, having a cup of tea, having kept his appointment. He looked very, very frazzled.

'Get that bike in the boot and stop being silly,' I said. He walked past me silently, nose in the air. When I went to the car he wasn't there. I drove out of the grounds across the Mansfield Road and there he stood on the grass verge having thought better of trying the return trip in his state. I lowered the passenger window as I drew alongside him to tell him to get in when I heard him mutter a word... you know the word he muttered, ladies, the one that men call us when they're angry with us! I drove on a few yards just to let him know I'd heard him, and that's when it escalated. He had to take it a stage further, a stage too far in fact and he shouted it again. However, this time he preceded that word, with another word that I know is very fashionable nowadays for all and sundry to use, even coming through our TVs into our living rooms. 'Oh, am I?' I thought – 'I'll show you how much of a one I can be' and put my foot down and drove off.

I looked in my mirror. I think if he had had two arms, he would have thrown his bike over the hedge in rage. Who decided that it would be OK to let language like that become fashionable to use, and to let that genie out of the bottle? Neither of us used that language, certainly never ever at each other. Not because we are holier than thou, it's just respect for each other and how we were bought up. When we were children if you had been heard using such a word by an adult you would have needed someone to sew your head back on your shoulders.

All this, I thought, over a blooming sleeping policeman? If it had been a real one, I could have understood it. I stopped halfway and considered going back. He could get knocked down - the roads once through Papplewick and Hucknall only had uneven grass verges so it would be difficult walking alongside a bike when he was unable to ride.

No, I thought, he's behaving like a child, and you know the old saying - spare the rod and spoil the child! He can walk if he can't ride.

I got home and spent the next two or three hours up and down the stairs looking for him out of the bedroom window and down the avenue, sick with worry, until he finally limped round the corner pushing his bike, looking completely wrecked. I shot downstairs, grabbed a newspaper and sat nonchalantly reading it when he walked in.

I said, 'You look shattered, would you like a cup of tea?'

'Oh please,' he replied, 'I could murder one' and that was that. Tantrum over and never mentioned again. Well, until now!

All these years later, whenever I hear Paul McCartney on the radio singing the song, 'A Long and Winding Road' I still think of that day.

CHAPTER 40

Ilkeston Junction

Ilkeston Junction was a little community all on its own.
Set alongside a busy little railway station, a pub called the Dew Drop Inn and a large hosiery factory, where hundreds of young women worked, some not much more than girls. There were scores of back-to-back terraced houses on about four or five streets.

It was a hard-working community, quite rough and ready, but very generous with what they had, even though it was usually very little. The Junction had a giant version of everything on their playground. Their rocking horse was bigger than any others in the area, their swings were higher and the see-saw longer, and their roundabout definitely went faster, especially when two or three tough young lads were trying to spin squealing girls off.

Ilkeston Junction

Kids would have to be very brave to venture down The Junction if they didn't belong to the neighbourhood though, because the kids were tough, and you would soon get bashed up.

I had no trouble blending in because I had a foot in both camps, so to speak. My grandad and grandma lived on Wentworth Street. Dad was raised there too, and my grandad's brother, Percy, lived on Digby Street. My grandad and his brother were twins, identical twins! This caused Grandad many problems because his brother was a drinker and a gambler, so he was often accosted by men wanting their money back that his brother owed them.

It got so bad that in the end Grandad grew a moustache to differentiate between them. His rascally brother, it was said, was often wheeled home from the Dewdrop in a wheelbarrow after imbibing too much. It's good to see the station open again, but that community to me was like an island set apart from everywhere else. Sadly, I've never seen anywhere quite like it since.

CHAPTER 41

First Meeting

As children, I think, we all believe childhood will never end. The six-week holiday stretching ahead of us at the end of July seemed unbelievably long, and still does for today's children.

The kids of my era were lucky enough to have the freedom to spend those long days roaming the district in a manner that would today have the police alerted within an hour of being out of their parents' sight! 'Make sure you're back for tea' would be the last instruction as you went out of the door in the morning, often clutching a younger sibling by the hand.

So, to suddenly find your schooldays had come to an end came, perhaps, not as a surprise (because most young people at that time couldn't wait to leave) but as a bit of a shock given the rapid entry into the workforce!

Many would start work within a week or two of leaving school, so you could forget about those long school holidays and there was no such phrase as a gap year then. You were expected to start work ASAP, and most kids would have as the saying went then, to 'tip up' at the end of the week. That meant you gave whatever you had earned (a paltry sum) to your mam or dad for your keep, much to the consternation of the new employee and a new-found bone of contention in the family. That would be before you were earning enough to pay board which was to be negotiated with your parents, many of whom did not take kindly to losing your wage so wanted as much of your new found wealth as they could get!

Most of the factories worked on the 'piece work' system and it encouraged everyone to work hard and to try and earn as much as possible. Everyone, I was told, kept their eye on each other when working piece work rates. No one wanted someone doing the same job to be earning more than they were so would soon be trying to keep up with the faster ones. Anyone who was earning more than the average would be labelled as 'grabbers' and often accused of taking others' work. You could walk past many factories, like perhaps Rutland Garments, and hear scores of machines going hell for leather. The noise, to those who walked by, was thunderous. Some did earn good money, but they certainly worked hard for it…

Jobs were plentiful in Ilkeston during that period and the town was buzzing. It was a brilliant shopping town with South Street and Bath Street full of thriving little shops. People would come from miles away to shop, many preferring it to the nearby city of Nottingham or Derby. Ilkeston Market was one of the best known in Derbyshire.

It came as a bit of a surprise to see my little sister, who had been a troublesome pain in the backside for most of my life and whose antics I had to endure, seemingly turn into a young woman overnight upon leaving school.

Having left at fifteen she started work as a trainee machinist and within a few months had miraculously transformed into an incredibly hard-working young woman. She was soon holding her own with much older women on piece work and was earning a pretty decent wage. With her new-found

independence and money in her pocket, she was soon stepping
into the start of the 'Swinging Sixties', dressed to kill in the latest fashion of
the era. Her bubbly personality made it easy for her to make lots of new
friends. She loved and fully embraced this new world as a working girl,
having never been enamoured with the rigidity of school life.

I remember well the first time she brought her first serious boyfriend home
to meet Mam and Dad. It was a beautiful, warm summer's day when they
walked in. Dad was standing on a stool changing a light bulb and the fire was
roaring up the chimney back as usual! It was never out (these were the days
prior to our present-day smokeless zones).

Dad, being a miner, received a coal allowance and he meant to burn it! There
was no way on God's earth that he would have surrendered a load back to
the Coal Board. 'I've earned every cobble', he vehemently defended, when
Mam complained about how much we had. You could only give so much
away and most of the men around us were miners who were in the same
boat.

Dad, as usual, had his jumper on! It didn't matter how hot it got he didn't
like removing it.

'Mam, Dad…' my sister said. 'This is Fred.'

Fred looked nervously up at my dad, who looked over his shoulder at him.
Dad then threw out his arm and in a loud Shakespearean voice, as if he was
some great orator on the stage of the Old Vic, looked Fred straight in the eye
and said, 'The boy stood on the burning deck, his pocket full of crackers, one
fell down between his legs…'

He never finished! Mam shouted, 'Gordon! Pack it in! Fred will think you're
mad.'

I think Fred did think it all a bit strange, but he continued to come. Years
later he confided to me that when my sister had been having one of her
awkward moments with him in the early days of courtship (like the time
after a spat she took all the new saucepans he had bought for her bottom

drawer and threw them down the entry on Chaucer Street were Fred lived) that it was often the sumptuous dinners and teas Mam used to put on every Sunday that kept him on track!

Fred was a calm, thoughtful young man who was not easily riled and proved to be a perfect match for my sister's hot-headed nature back in her youth. They have now been very happily married for 57 years and blessed with two lovely boys, five wonderful grandchildren and a great-grandchild. Thankfully, Fred's initial meeting with dad didn't put him off!

So, my sister's wonderful childhood had come to an abrupt end but thanks to a time when jobs were plentiful and our town thrived, she had a good working life ahead of her, interrupted for a time bringing up her children that soon arrived after getting married. I wish her and Fred, many more happy years in retirement, surrounded by family and the many wonderful friends they have made in our town.

First Meeting

CHAPTER 42

The Mechanical Horse

Most of the goods and parcels coming into Ilkeston and many towns in the UK up until the mid sixties came in by rail. Trains would run into Ilkeston North goods depot on Heanor road, opposite to where Ilkeston police station is now. New houses have been built on the site now.

Horses and drays (wagons) would also carry goods into the town from the Town Station situated were Tesco is now, with stables extending down Rutland Street. This served the town right into the 1950s. My father-in-law told us that in the early fifties, Barton's had some clapped-out petrol buses and the drivers would think it amusing to turn the ignition off and back on whilst the bus was moving. This resulted in a very loud explosion and a big cloud of black smoke being left behind the bus. He said a horse and dray was delivering to the Co-op painting and decorating shop, that was, at that time, practically opposite where the buses left the market, when a bus driver decided to perform this prank.

There was a terrific explosion, a cloud of smoke and the horse promptly bolted, putting the shafts of the dray through the plate glass window. He said there was the devil to pay about it. These antics were stopped after that with threats of immediate dismissal for any driver caught doing it.

I don't really know when horses ceased to be used completely by British Rail in Ilkeston. They were eventually replaced with three-wheeled articulated vehicles with a long trailer. These could be unhitched and left behind at the depot for goods loading whilst the driver could hitch onto another trailer that was loaded and ready for delivery. Sometimes when the trailers were fully loaded at the depot on Heanor Road for delivery to some large factory or merchant, they would be dropped and left at the premises for their staff to unload and the empty trailer collected later.

This was a well-practised and efficient way of keeping the busy shops and factories of Ilkeston ticking over. There were other small carriers delivering goods on a much smaller scale, of course, but British Rail was the mainstay. There was a very old-fashioned looking three-wheeler that used to run around Ilkeston in the fifties. It was a pretty tired, beat up and noisy old thing. I had the impression that the doors were made of wood, but this could well be my imagination! These red and cream lorries with a starting handle at the front had a gleaming brass plate with the words 'Scammel Mechanical Horse' inscribed upon it. You would sometimes hear boys making up quiz games or testing their friends with the question, 'where can you find a mechanical horse in Ilkeston?' It probably interested me because there was a mechanical horse story in one of my comics of the time. The plate on the Ilkeston one shone like gold in the sunlight - clearly some driver's pride and joy - polished regularly and cared for; perhaps it was this that caught my eye...

These were later replaced by the more modern 'Scammel Scarab', another three-wheeled articulator. The small 'three tonners' were usually grossly overloaded, and you would often see them struggling to get up Bath Street, with the engine roaring in a very low gear. But these six or seven little lorries kept Ilkeston, Heanor and Eastwood's shops, businesses, farms and factories supplied with goods, parcels and cattle feed (Langley Mill had its own station, depot and van.)

Sadly, Dr Beeching, who was brought in to make British Rail more efficient and profitable, put an end to all that by closing stations and axing lines. Ilkeston would have a long wait to get its railway station back after its closure in 1964. The result of the rail cuts meant many more vehicles having to transport goods by road all over the country. I often wonder if those distribution depots had remained open, whether they would be as efficient now as they were then, impossible without the rail link to them of course.

The little three-wheeled vehicles were ideal for even the narrowest of side streets as they could spin on that one front wheel and turn in half their own length. They were not just used by British Rail. Many large companies across the UK used them for local deliveries and yard duties, finding them ideal for the narrow alleyways of the yards. I read somewhere the military also used them in depots across the country. People who worked at Players can perhaps remember their little articulator, and I was told British Celanese at Spondon had one.

We also had the station at Ilkeston Junction which had its own large van delivering parcels and packages round the area. Mr Tetley was the driver there for many years and Mr Mather was the Station Master in charge of Ilkeston North station and the goods depot situated across the other side of the road. He was a very smart, polite man in his navy-blue suit and peaked hat with gold braid on the brim. He ran his station very efficiently and the staff took great pride in keeping the station very clean with window boxes on show in the summer.

It must have been heartbreaking for them when it closed. Trains ran on time and we could ride to Derby Friar Gate, quickly and cheaply.

Some readers might have seen the photographs that were displayed upstairs in the library, of Mr Mather with the Mayor and press inspecting Ilkeston North and surrounding stations' vehicles in the annual 'Best Kept Vehicles Competition.' Many Ilkeston people must be very pleased to have

eventually got their station back after much campaigning and lobbying and there must also be many people who have been pleasantly surprised at the popularity the station is enjoying.

It is good to see it back, at last.

CHAPTER 43

Pye Bridge Station: The Goat Story

Mr David Kirk, Ex-Station Master

I was appointed to the position of Booking and Parcels clerk at Pye Bridge station in September 1954, just three months short of my seventeenth birthday and I remained there until I was called for National Service in the Royal Army Pay Corps in May 1956. It was a two-shift job, early turn from 07:00 and late turn from 13:00 and my colleague on the other shift was Mr Ted Denslow, who lived at Selston and who had been amongst the troops evacuated from the beaches of Dunkirk in 1940.

The principal duties were issuing tickets for the train services, dealing with passenger enquiries and dealing with forwarded and received parcels traffic. There was also internal office work in connection with the calculation of staff pay, payment arrangements each week and other correspondence. The parcels side was always busy with customers bringing parcels for despatch

and collecting parcels which had arrived.

In 1954 and early 1955 the railways were classed as "Common Carriers" which was a relic from Victorian days, but it meant that the railways had to accept almost anything for despatch on the system. This was changed by decree in either late 1955 or early 1956. The story that follows is before this major change.

I was on the early turn at the station one morning when I saw a small road van arrive outside the parcels office, the van was owned by "Pooleys" who provided weighing machines and weighbridges etc for the railways. The driver came in and told me that he had brought the new weighing machine for the parcels office, and he needed to set it up. This he did, it was of a type which I had not seen before but he explained and demonstrated to me how it was to be operated, tested me on my operation and once he was satisfied, he then gave me a fairly large, stiff card which set out all the details as previously explained to me. He said that it needed to be displayed on the wall behind the weighing machine so that any staff could read this and operate the machine in accordance with the instructions.

After he had gone, I attached this thick card to a nail in the wall in the designated place.

Shortly after, I had my first customer. It was a farmer or one of his employees who walked up the road leading a goat on a rope. He brought it into the parcels office and told me that it was to go to Clay Cross on the next train. This was no problem; the goat would travel in the guard's van and would be handed over to the station staff at Clay Cross on arrival. It was, of course, necessary to raise the carriage charge for this and this meant that the goat needed to be weighed. This was easier said than done as it meant that the goat had to be positioned on the weigh platform and it was in no way interested in that. Matters were not helped by me laughing helplessly at our combined efforts to manoeuvre the goat's legs onto the platform, we were both pulling and tugging, I was laughing and the farmer was blaspheming (probably at me as well as the goat.)

After what seemed like a long time, we finally managed to get the goat positioned and I stepped forward to operate the machine. I checked on the instructions which I had posted earlier on the wall only to see the last vestige of them in the goat's mouth which he was chewing so very happily. I managed to weigh the goat eventually, attach a parcel stamp to the label and off it went on its way. I was left with the new weighing machine and no operating instructions. A few hours later, to my relief, Mr Denslow arrived, and I demonstrated the new machine to him.

He said, 'where are the instructions?' and of course I had to tell him that the goat had eaten them. His reply? Totally unprintable.

To complete this little story, a couple of years ago I visited the Great Central Railway at Loughborough and there on the platform I saw an identical weighing machine on display. It brought it all back to me to see this.

CHAPTER 44

Full Circle

Life's Little Ups and Downs

I would just like remind readers that these stories were recalled and written to amuse my family. The ones written now about adult life are especially what I wanted to leave to our son and daughter, to put away and perhaps look at later with our two grandsons when they are older so that they can see a little of what Mama and Grandad were once like, to amuse them and perhaps not always just remember me as an old lady in her chair struggling to speak.

I never ever thought the stories would be shown to other people; it was all pure chance, so if we appear more than a little foolish sometimes, well that's what you share with your family, and I don't mind sharing with you.

Betty, 2023

The photograph shown above is one of the last taken with my friends at Hallcroft before we all went our various ways into the working world or on to further study.

I went on to teacher training at the Bath Academy of Art. My dad and grandma took me to Bath for my interview. I was very nervous and what a journey! We left Ilkeston by train very early in the morning for Friargate Station, Derby and from there we caught another bus to the main Derby Station. We changed at Birmingham, stopping it seemed at every station from Derby to Bath. It was early afternoon before we arrived. We had another bus ride to the Academy. My interview was with the Chancellor and two tutors, and they seemed to want to know everything about me. They went through my portfolio of work, quizzing me about this, that and the other. I felt like a wrung-out dishcloth when they finally finished with me, they thanked me for coming and said they would be in touch.

We returned very slowly to Derby and arrived late evening to thick fog, a real pea-souper. Everything had stopped, the station had closed, no buses were running, and we were stranded! My Grandma was very tired, and we were worried about her. She shouldn't have come but had insisted, wanting to know whether or not where I was going was suitable. The Station Master came and summed up the situation, opened the waiting room for us and lit a fire that was soon up the chimney back with a bucket of coal by the side to keep it topped up. Dad used it all through that long night and we were all soon nice and warm. The Station Master then returned with a tray with mugs of tea for us (cup and saucer for Grandma) and biscuits. What a nice man!

We spent the night in the waiting room and after the best night's sleep she'd had for ages, Grandma said, 'I think that was mainly due to the rhythmic rumble of goods trains passing through the station through the night.' Grandma and Grandad had lived for years, when younger, on Wentworth Street at The Junction close to the railway track and old memories resurfaced, plus she wasn't used to being fussed over. Another cup of tea from our friendly Station Master next morning and we caught a bus to Friargate Station when the fog finally lifted, then it was back home on the short ride from Friargate to Ilkeston.

I was accepted for a place and my dad waved me off (with my trunk and bike stored in the guard's van.) I phoned him on the second day I was there and told him I wanted to come home. It was the first time I had been away from my family overnight. My dad called me back from the telephone box at the bottom of Alvenor Street and told me to give it a while longer. I had no choice anyway, as I hadn't got the train fare home.

It was a pretty strict regime at Bath and not at all like the freedom today's students have. You could get sent down for any number of infractions that would be laughable by today's standards but I came to love my years there. When qualified, my first post was Bennerley, which I also came to love; great pupils and staff. I resigned when I became pregnant but if I had continued working, I could have afforded to put our new baby into a nursery. This was never even considered by either of us as paid maternity leave had not been rolled out and most women like me were of the mindset that you stayed at home and looked after your baby. Today, with so many good nurseries, I would be of a different opinion considering the excellent social skills the infants gain.

We soon found, like many young people with a mortgage, a new baby and just one wage coming in, that things were a little tight, to say the least so I was very pleased to get a part-time post at Hallcroft co-ed secondary school in Ilkeston. My old school!

It was a peculiar sensation walking back through the gates of my old school early on my first day as a staff member there instead of a pupil and going to the staff room to be introduced to the rest of the staff. They welcomed me like an old friend, already forewarned no doubt by Miss Severn, the deputy head, of my appointment.

My head of department was a Mr Nix, a lovely, talented man from whom I learned a great deal and Mr Smith, the other member of our team. I had immense respect for these two men, great colleagues, and later friends: perfect gentlemen, the pair of them.

I enjoyed the years I taught at Hallcroft. My mum looked after our baby son and I was working a part-time post, which suited me down to the ground. I loved Hallcroft and working with my colleagues, many of whom had taught me when I was a pupil there. When our son was due to start school, I had tried to get him in to Chaucer Infants which would have been the icing on the cake. We lived in Awsworth, just over the border in Nottinghamshire but I was informed that I couldn't have a child educated in another county to the one I lived in. We even considered selling up and moving to Ilkeston. The rules must have changed later because my daughter went to an Ilkeston school, no problem, although perhaps not; she went to St John Houghton, a Catholic school, which would make a difference.

Things then began to get difficult, with my needing to work in the afternoons so that I could take our son to Awsworth Infants in the mornings.

Timetables had to be juggled to accommodate afternoons working at Hallcroft so a regular taxi had to be booked to pick our son up from Awsworth School to take him down to my mum's in Ilkeston at the end of his school day until I could walk down to collect him from Blake Street when I finished work.

Sometimes the slightly different holidays, half term breaks etc. between Nottinghamshire and Derbyshire where I worked could cause me problems but the Head, Mr Nash and later Mr Waller, and Mr Nix had no issues about me bringing our son into school to sit in with my classes, where he was often fussed over by the girls who were all most helpful and considerate. I don't think I would get away with that nowadays so happy days for me.

However when Mr Nix, my Head of Department, left suddenly, my very comfortable happy time at Hallcroft changed somewhat. I was asked if I was interested in applying for the full-time post that was left by Mr Nix but I declined saying I was very comfortable working part-time. Having a small son it gave me a more flexible working life, apart from the fact that if I had got the job, I wouldn't have been able to fully commit myself to it, with our small son to consider and unable to drive at that time.

Michael, my husband, went into a bit of a tailspin, thinking of the very substantial increase in salary that the job would have brought in and bravely offered to stay home and become a house husband. I declined his offer. His idea of having dinner on ready for me if I was late home was four or five peeled potatoes in a pan of cold water. He had also failed miserably on the nappy changing front when our son was younger. I told him 'On your bike, Mike, if anyone's staying home it's me!'

My new Head of Department and I unfortunately did not get on together quite so well, so when several years later there were education cuts across the country, many part-time posts were axed including mine. I was not at all as sad as I would have been at one time apart from, that is, leaving behind treasured friends and colleagues, most of whom I never saw again even though I was local. I had no call to go back to the school, although I did keep in touch with one colleague who now lives in Scotland. We only exchange Christmas cards these adays and I haven't seen her for years.

Little could I have imagined that Friday afternoon, when I walked with my bits and bobs in a box in my arms out of the gates of Hallcroft, a place that had been so important in my life for so many years, for what would be the very last time. It would be years before I returned to the job I loved but soon we would be blessed with a wonderful daughter. Then a completely different working life awaited me and a career change that I could never have guessed but that was an absolute life saver for me, and only a couple of hundred yards away from where I was standing.

CHAPTER 45

Fate's Fickle Finger

Life's Little Ups and Downs

Part 1

I was very happy teaching at Hallcroft, and life was good. I had a kind, loving and hard-working husband and my mother and father-in-law, Bernard and Dora, were a lovely couple and my mum and dad were, at that time, in reasonable health. I couldn't have wished for better.

My father-in-law's parents, Matilda and Jim, were also a much loved and important part of the family. Michael and I would spend nice weekends with them in their cottage in Mountsorrel, which is between Loughborough and Leicester. To top it all we had a little boy, Patrick, who was worshipped by the whole family. He was a very happy, easy-going child and we hoped he would eventually be joined by a brother or sister. Life was good.

I have always been a fatalist, believing it only takes one small event to change the course of things completely. The butterfly effect. And so, it was with us. Perhaps we were tempting fate with our blissful happiness? Our lives were soon to change in the blink of an eye.

Michael's much-loved grandmother, Matilda, died suddenly at their home in Mountsorrel. It was unexpected. She had always been very healthy, so it was an enormous shock to us all. We attended her funeral six days later, wearily and sadly returning home that evening. It had been a long and stressful day, and I made a meal for Bernard, Dora and ourselves. We were all bereft and afterwards they left for home. The last thing Bernard said to me as he left was, 'I've never felt so tired in my life, Betty.' I put it down to him losing his mum and the strains of the day.

In the early hours of the next morning, we were awoken by our neighbour, who was banging on the front door. We didn't have a land line at this time, so messages were conveyed through her number.

'Michael you have to go up to your mum's straight away. Your dad's ill.' My husband rushed to Cotmanhay only to find his mum weeping and his dad dead on the living room floor. His father had just turned fifty-one.

We were all shocked, broken and grieving but Dora soon had to return to work at Chambers Factory, opposite Trinity Church. Life was tough.

A short while later education cuts took their toll, and I was made redundant from Hallcroft. Michael was trying his best to morally support everyone. He worked very long hours himself, but whenever he could he was up at his mum's trying to console her and give her support.

His grandfather, Jim, also needed support and help. He did not have a wide circle of friends, having only recently moved from London. It was an hour's travel for Michael to get to Mountsorrel and his grandad would expect him to spend two or three hours with him before he left for home again. The expectation from him was that Michael would do this two or three times a week. There just didn't seem to be enough hours in the day and my poor husband was running himself ragged and I was beginning to worry he would crack up.

Life was soon to take another turn… despite a slight inkling that something was about to happen, I didn't dare dwell on it or really consider what was sitting uneasily at the back of my mind. Or should I say, what was at the back of my husband's. Surely things couldn't get any worse…?

Michael had worked for P&O, the shipping company, during his late teens and early twenties, on their cruise liners. So, when I noticed letters arriving in P&O envelopes, I began to get an uneasy feeling. I hadn't the courage to ask of their contents and he didn't say. I chose ostrich tactics and buried my head. Life was difficult enough without making waves.

One fine morning, my husband announced he was taking myself and our young son on a day trip to London later in the week. This was a nice surprise for us and a much-needed break, although somewhat unexpected especially as money was tight. We were both mentally exhausted.

It was a lovely sunny day and we left early. After a fun time watching the changing of the guard at Buckingham Palace, we set off to the Bloody Tower. A large, fancy ice cream cone with chocolate sprinkles was the order of the day for each of us afterwards, bought from a van outside the Tower.

No expense was spared that day even if Michael did moan that the vendor was a 'blooming robber' (we had our picnic packed up for later of course!)

As we strolled through London, Michael suddenly announced he had to go somewhere and 'shouldn't be too long'. He left us alone to board HMS Belfast, the WW2 cruiser moored on the Thames, for a guided tour. 'Crikey!', I thought to myself, 'he's pushing the boat out for us today. I wonder where he's gone?'

With surprises coming thick and fast I could only assume it was another he had planned. How right I turned out to be…

Patrick and I had a great time exploring the ship, which he stills recalls. He loved it, relishing looking at the big guns and running up and down the deck where a sailor chatted to him about the ship.

Michael met us later that afternoon and indeed another surprise was imminent. He revealed that he had just returned from the Shipping Federation and re- joined the Seaman's Union. His Seaman's Discharge book had been updated and he was going back into the Merchant Navy. P&O were welcoming him back with open arms. Mine were staying firmly crossed. To say that this put a bit of a damper on the day was an understatement. It was a very quiet journey back up the M1 at fifty miles an hour in our old banger. It would have taken more than a cornet and a trip round an old warship to sweeten me that day.

I didn't try to dissuade him though and nor did his mother. We weren't happy about it, but we knew he was not in a good place. He was grieving too and trying to make things right for everyone else, which of course he couldn't.

Within two weeks he was gone! He sailed away from Southampton on one of P&O's luxury ships, the SS Oriana, to cruise around the Mediterranean. He was not expected back for months.

My lovely life had come crashing down around my ears, seemingly destroyed forever. I was okay, of course. Lonely and unhappy but I reminded myself a lot of people were worse off. I had Michael's wages coming in every month, a nice house and our little boy to look after. Things could be worse… and seemingly would be later!

It was great seeing him come home on leave some months later looking healthy, tanned and more like his old self. He said he was leaving again in a couple of weeks, off to Australia to cruise around the Pacific. He had also been promoted with the prospect of much more money.

Life was pretty miserable for me. I lived, and still do, in a nice cul-de-sac and everyone over the years has been wonderful but no-one lived in each other's pockets (thank goodness.) I had no close friends as such and looked forward to going down to my see my mam, dad and sister's family, who gathered at my parents on a Saturday and to my mother-in-law's house on Sundays.

Michael had been gone for months and I wrote to every port they arrived at on the itinerary and 'red lined' his arrival through on the calendar, looking forward to the day I crossed off the last one and he would be back home.

We had a giant world map pinned up in our son's bedroom, carefully plotting the voyages of Daddy's ship. Michael replied to all my letters and seemed very happy. He had a job he couldn't have dreamt of not so long ago. He worked in the first-class restaurant on the Oriana and was the supervisor to twenty staff. In the evenings he was a wine waiter himself - selling wine to the 320 passengers in his section. Cash was king at this time and credit cards not used. Cash changed hands for everything throughout the ship from the Captain and Purser down. Tipping was the natural order of the day for staff in these sections from the first-class clientele. I was sitting having breakfast one morning after taking my son to school when my world took a second hit. The postman left our mail and I picked a letter up addressed to 'Mrs O'Neal', my name misspelt, from Australia. 'Who is this from?' I wondered. 'I don't know anyone from Australia apart from Michael and this isn't from him.'

I opened the envelope and stood, rooted to the floor, with shock. Two photographs were inside. Nothing else.

They were innocent enough to anyone else, but not to me at that time. One of the photos had Michael sitting under blue skies on the deck of his ship on a luxury lounger, his arms around two beautiful bikini clad Aussie girls who sat perched upon on each knee. He had a big cheesy grin on his face. The other was in the restaurant where he was working, planted in the midst of a group of young women who all looked very friendly. A little too friendly and too demonstrative for my liking. A saucy message was scribbled on the back of each of the pictures for good measure. I sat at the table and had a good cry for the rest of the morning and repeated over and over the same word I thought about him. It was later that evening I chose to scrawl that same word across the front of the envelope of the letter I had written to him. I was gutted. How could I compete with those bikini clad girls? I hadn't even got a bikini, only an old swimsuit; no luxury lounger, only an old deck chair his mum had given us to put on our lawn (which badly needed cutting.) I showed the photos to his mum. I can't repeat what she said.

I sent him a scorching letter with the two photographs inside and perhaps, after one or two glasses of cider that night, I upgraded his rank to bar steward. Something like that anyway. It was the word I'd kept repeating to myself which I scrawled across the front of the envelope in large letters - by then my hurt had turned to rage. This amused many of his shipmates who saw the addressed envelope at the ship's crew mail office before he got round to collecting it.

He was most concerned and phoned me as soon as he could at his mum's. He had, he said, been the victim of a prank that had been going on for some time and all the crew had been warned about leaving personal information lying around. It was thought young Aussie passengers were responsible.

And the photographs? 'Nothing' he said. It was part of his job to wander around his section making sure the passengers had everything they wanted, and many became friends during the cruises. 'I have lots of pictures taken with people every day', he said. 'Some get passed over to me. I'll show you some when I get home.' (Hmmm!).
'You should know you can trust me,' he said. I replied at the time, 'Even

Adam and Eve had succumbed when in Paradise and tempted by a juicy
apple!' When he eventually arrived home, I knew there was more to come.

'What now?!' I sighed 'Oh', he said, 'I have signed on again and we are going
to be cruising round the Norwegian Fjords to see the Northern Lights before
we head off back to Australia'.
'Well whilst you are up there', I said calmly, 'you had better build yourself an
igloo, because you are going to need somewhere to live when you have
finished gallivanting!'
Michael got the message and time was called on his little adventures at sea.
He went back, unsigned himself, collected his gear and came home. He
never got to see the Northern Lights!

Part 2
The Real World

I never regretted making Michael come home. It was a dream job and
existence for him (especially after such trauma and grief) but it was
incompatible with family life.
We then made a big mistake, one which I must admit to encouraging. When
I was unpacking his baggage, I opened a case which was full of money! Rolls
of it in different currencies. 'Oh my God! What did you do? Rob a bank?!' I
squealed. 'Oh no', he laughed, 'It's only tips and commission from wine
accumulated over the months. I just threw it in my case every night when I
finished work. I didn't really know what else to do with it.'
He had worked relentlessly for seven days a week for months and months.
So, on his return he decided to have a little break instead of getting a job. I
encouraged him, knowing it would be good for us as a family. The break
though lasted over a year! He didn't sign on, knowing he was fit for work and
that this was his choice. Any bills which needed to be paid he said, 'Oh get
some from the case.' That was until one day I opened the case and found just
one lonely roll of dollars and Japanese yen.

'The money's all gone!' I cried. Panic stations ensued! He had to get a job
and quickly. My sister's husband, Fred, worked at the Raleigh bike factory in
Nottingham. His foreman was Harry Hardy, well known in Ilkeston as the

oldest football referee still playing. Fred had a word with Harry, and they fixed Michael up with a job. Fred still laughs now about the day Michael turned up for his first shift. He had never worked in a factory before and the workshop he was going into was incredibly hot, noisy and smelly, with everyone working 'hell for leather.'

I had sent him off in the same way he had always gone to work - neatly pressed white shirt, a tie, smart jacket and his 'snap' in a Tupperware container. Fred gleefully recalls how they thought it was someone from senior management arriving for a tour!

They put him on something called the 'Riggs', a large welding machine. My husband described it to me as 'something designed by a sadist to break the spirit of the strongest man.' He said he would press a button and the machine would start welding a bike frame at half a dozen different points.

He would press the button to start the welding, walk back to the first machine and take off the completed one. Ad infinitum. Or for at least an eight hour shift anyway… He said he could see his brother-in-law, Fred, who had got him the job, grinning at him at the end of his little walkway. My husband admitted he had thought the same about Fred for getting him that job as I had about him when the photographs from Australia landed through the door! My husband's slight, nine stone, self-slumped home from his first shift that evening looking like a limp lettuce.

Fred quietly said to him as they left that evening 'Welcome to the real world, Michael.'

He didn't last long in that department before he moved to another and eventually got trained up as a Quality Control Technician. He moved to the Trowel Toy division where he was much more at home, wandering around, checking the work the ladies were turning out and no doubt gossiping away the day. He admits he was much better at telling people what to do than doing it himself. Life had returned to something resembling normality again and we were both overjoyed to discover I was expecting a baby. I eventually gave birth to a perfect and beautiful baby girl. Nothing could spoil that.

Could it...?

CHAPTER 46

A Bit of a Change

Life's Little Ups and Downs

It turned out to be a fortuitous time to leave my teaching post at Hallcroft as I fell pregnant and eventually gave birth to my beautiful daughter. My mother wouldn't have been fit enough to look after our new daughter even if I had still been working. Our new addition to the family was pretty demanding and seemed to be permanently welded to my hip for a few years. I became adept at cooking with one hand for the pans and one for the baby (I blame her for my having to have them both replaced later!)

She slept poorly as she wasn't allowed into our bed because Michael, my husband, had to be up early. The nights were long as I spent them awake trying to pacify her so he could get his sleep and be in a state to work the next day. Of course, this is the bane of mothers with new babies the world over but unfortunately our little treasure had a real problem with being separated from me for even the shortest of time, even to being put down into her pram or cot for a while. After a little time, I began to have the same problem, worrying what kind of state she was getting herself into if I was missing whenever she woke up. This had been going on for some time and lack of sleep and a little post-natal depression took its toll on me.

It had been my decision to give up my career. I'd wanted children and I wanted to be at home for them through those first years. That was my choice. Other people felt differently and that was theirs. We all try to make the right decisions for our own circumstances. Our only problem was this separation issue that our daughter had. It was really serious, and it wasn't healthy. My husband, the GP and I all felt I needed to be away from her for a little at a time, gradually building it up. This would give me a break and gradually get our baby used to me not being there all the time. It was a very difficult time. If I could have left her for a while and broken this separation anxiety our daughter had, I would have. It would have been great for both of us, but it was very difficult, and it took her first few years to achieve.

Then out of the blue I was informed that a post had become vacant at Ilkeston Grammar School. I didn't want to go back to even part-time work; that wasn't part of the plan. I had two children and I wanted them to have those precious early years with me. I wasn't pressured into applying for the post, my husband was a hard-working man and a good provider, but we were the same as many other people bringing up a family and money was tight. I was tempted. Michael had found a nice lady just up the road who was in a similar situation to me. She had a young child too and was looking forward to earning a wage looking after our daughter if I got the job.

Michael took me to the interview as I didn't drive at that time. We left our daughter with my apprehensive mother-in-law (who knew my daughter's rages well!) Typically, because I really didn't want a full-time job, the interview went great guns. I knew the area art organiser from my previous posts and we got on very well, both knowing colleagues in Ilkeston schools. I came away thinking despondently that it was pretty obvious that they were going to offer me the post and I really didn't feel well enough or even want to do it.

We got home to find my mother-in-law frazzled and our daughter in a terrible state after barely a couple of hours. I immediately phoned the school and withdrew my application. It wouldn't have been fair to the lady who wanted to look after our child or to risk our child driving someone to distraction and possibly being harmed. The interviewer was very disappointed but I was relieved. As far as I was concerned my career was on hold for the foreseeable future. How to try to get a little time for myself was the issue. Michael wasn't helping the situation; he was the only one she would spend a little more time with and even with him she started fretting pretty quickly.

He took on more hours and was working hard at the Raleigh bike factory in Nottingham from 7.30am to 4.30pm. He would be up at 6.30am and cycle from Awsworth across the bridleway and footpaths to Strelley Village and then down into Nottingham. He would get back home at around quarter past five, have his dinner and a quick shower then cycle back the same way to Skills bus depot in Nottingham and drive one of their coaches until 11.30pm, cycling back home the same way.

I would sit waiting for him, worrying that he might not come home in one piece. He was cycling back in the dark through the bridleways and footpaths, it was madness. He would laugh and say 'Don't be ridiculous. I can do it with my eyes shut!' He was desperately tired anyway with what was going on throughout the night with the baby. It was literally all bed and work for him, and we hardly saw each other. He said he was only doing it to keep the PSV licence he held current and up to date. 'You never know what's round the corner,' he'd say. The licence is a job in my pocket if ever I should need it.' At the time I couldn't help thinking that he wanted to go off and play with big boys' toys again (the fancy buses that he liked driving) or that he was just getting out of the way of all the screaming and meltdowns at home that seemed to go on endlessly day and night. So, I was determined, by hook or by crook, to put an end to this nonsense before there was an accident.

When he came home one day, I had a surprise for him. 'I've got a little job,' I said, 'but you will be in charge of the kids in the evening'. 'Doing what?' he said. 'Scrubbing out the Co-op butchery on South Street in the evenings. I start Monday evening, so you can pack that stupid job in now.' His lip came out. 'What have you got that face on for?' I said.

So, on the next Monday evening I met my new workmates, the half dozen ladies in tabards and turbans armed with mops buckets and dusters who were responsible for the cleaning of the Co-op from top to bottom every evening six days a week, under the eagle eye of Nola, the supervisor, responsible for the Co-op being kept spick and span. I was issued with my new uniform, a blue tabard, mop bucket, a large electric scrubber that had a mind of its own, a bag of cleaning cloths and then put to work. I was a little dismayed when I saw what awaited me. I had the toughest and most unenviable job on the team (I thought). The floors and walls of the butchery were sometimes very greasy and bloody, to put it mildly, and it wasn't long before I became a vegetarian and have been ever since. It was hard work but, with a quick walk back to Awsworth for me after work if the weather was fine, I could pop in to see if Mam and Dad were alright. It was just what I needed to get a bit of the outside world and to get my head in the right place and to get myself fit again. It did me good working with those big-hearted ladies who were always laughing or moaning about having extra work put on them and who welcomed me into their ranks with no nasty asides or barbs about my previous employment (which I had expected.) A couple of the girls' husbands had been former pupils, and they were all lovely. Well, not quite true, my husband always had some remark about my low wage and me being just a butcher's dog – oh no, a dog's male, isn't it? Of course, it was the other one!

I stayed at the Co-op for two or three years and really enjoyed it, looking forward all day to my two or three hours of freedom every evening.

When he came home one day, I surprised him again. 'I'm leaving the Co-op - I've got another little job', I said. 'Oh, why? What about our daughter?' he said, immediately concerned. 'Oh, don't worry, I've got a good minder.' 'Who?' he said. 'You!' I replied. 'You will still be in charge of the kids in the evenings.' 'Doing what? He said. 'I'm going to work for a solicitor's firm,' I replied. He was impressed 'Oh right!' he beamed. 'Are they going to train you up?' 'No,' I said, 'I'm able to go straight in and start work, I'm their new cleaner.' His lip came out. 'What have you got that face on again for?' I said. 'It's just what I want. It's close by and still only for two or three hours in the evenings, do you think you can cope?' It will be good for our young daughter and good for me.' 'Can I cope?' he said, 'It's me she's dealing with. She will be tucked up in bed fast asleep for when you get back.' I thought, 'good luck with that mate!'

I didn't mind the work at all. In fact, I think for those precious two or three hours to myself I would have paid my new employers to let me do it. I worked with just one other lady; she was very nice and friendly but working separately we saw little of each other. The work was easy and a little better paid but I did miss the laughs and banter of the ladies at the Co-op. I grew up with our Mam constantly cleaning in the forties and fifties. There were no gadgets really back then and Mam always had jobs for us to do so my new job was a piece of cake. It was a quick walk back to Awsworth for me after work, if the weather was fine, and still being able to nip in to see if my mam and dad were both ok was just what I needed. Those two or three hours helped me to get my head in the right place again during a very trying and difficult time in our lives and, as an added bonus, I got myself fit again. It really did me good getting out and working for a couple of hours.

Being unable to drive and not really wanting to learn limited me considerably for getting around quickly, which could be a nuisance.

Like many women I was well used to getting on buses loaded with bags, a couple of children and a pushchair. It was normal. So, it was great to be back standing at a bus stop by myself or in a queue as I did every evening, chatting to the people who would be catching the bus at the same time every evening on their way to work or wherever. That was how it was for most of us growing up. Most people travelled by bus to school, to work, or to get out and about. Believe it or not it was a treasured part of your social life, chatting to people who you had become used to travelling with.

Little did I imagine that one day pretty soon, on my return from work, my husband was going to be responsible for giving me such a nasty shock. All would change, and I would soon feel the need to be able to drive and to give myself more mobility and the ability to get back home as quickly as possible.

It was one fine summer's evening as I strolled home from work enjoying the last of the sun, I ran into every parent's worst nightmare. The sight of my husband pedalling furiously up the hill on his bike towards me, him looking and shouting down people's driveways panicked me. I started running towards him. 'What's the matter?' I shouted. 'I can't find her!' he cried back. 'She's gone (meaning our then four year-old daughter.) 'She was on the lawn playing, I only took my eyes off of her for a couple of minutes.'

'FIND HER!' I yelled at him as he pedalled past. I too frantically started shouting her name, running down the street to our house where I looked in wardrobes and under beds in a blind panic. He came back ten minutes later.

'Have you found her?' he shouted from the top of the drive. 'No,' I shouted, 'phone the police'. He pedalled off frantically again, returning five minutes later wheeling his bike and carrying our daughter, who was crying, on his arm. 'You'll kill me!' I shouted as my body flooded with both relief and anger. It turned out she had gone around the corner with her friend of a similar age, and they had become engrossed in watching a man take an engine out of his car. 'Daddy shouted at me!' she sobbed. 'Did he? Well, darling, I'm going to shout at him now too!' I told her.

That drama more than anything motivated me to do something about my mobility issues which had blighted my life. 'I want to learn to drive,' I said after calming down. 'I want to get from A to B quickly in future if you can't be trusted!'

'Is it my fault if she decides to go walkabout?' he said.

'She's four,' I yelled at him.

'If you want to drive, there's no need for us to pay for lessons, lass, I'll teach you.' he replied.

Why did this not surprise me?

'I know as much about driving as any instructor. All you need is a little patience.'

What could possibly go wrong?

CHAPTER 47

The Beetle

Life's Little Ups and Downs

The drama of a family emergency more than anything motivated me to do something about my mobility problem, or lack of it. Not being able to drive was blighting my life.

'I want to learn to drive,' I declared to my husband. Well of course I didn't need to go to driving school (or get the opportunity.)
'I'll teach you, lass,' my husband told me. 'No problem. No instructor knows more than I do!'

By this time, we had 'upgraded' to an old VW Beetle and so began an enduring love-hate relationship between us and the Beetle. This particular 'boneshaker' was, to put it mildly, very temperamental. She would stop for no apparent reason, even after three new (well, nearly new) engines. Often, she wouldn't start if she didn't feel like it. It was freezing cold in the winter with the heater barely capable of mustering the warmth of a candle.

After numerous occasions upon which our beloved jalopy failed to start, we would resort to hitting the starter motor with a hammer (kept in the engine compartment for such eventualities.) We finally discovered the reason for her repeated ignition failure. Our Beetle had a six-volt battery located somewhere under the back seat. By the time the power from the little battery had been through the wiring to reach the ignition there wasn't enough power left to start her. The local VW specialist cannily fitted a starter button in the middle of the panel in the front of the leg room of the back seat. Having wired it up to the starter motor directly below it in the rear engine compartment, it solved the problem. It just left one small peculiarity. The driver could only start the car by simply putting their left arm between the front seats and feeling for the starter button. This caused a little consternation some years later when Michael went to pick up our daughter from the Girl Guides on a dark, rainy evening. Her friends all piled into the back with her. My husband's arm and hand suddenly appeared between the seats. 'It's okay,' our daughter said, 'he's looking for the starter button!'

'I think I'd better pick them up from Guides in future before you get into trouble!' I said.

My husband and I have never had a stand-up row in fifty-five years. We never raise our voices towards each other (unless our daughter goes missing of course.)

Both of us could be a little hot tempered in our younger years. Still, we were always aware that once something was said or shouted, it can't be unsaid. So instead of raging at each other like normal people and clearing the air we would have 'quiet periods.' OK, we sulked! Until one of us relented and apologised for the thing we had both forgotten about by then. Unfortunately, these quiet spells could be rather difficult when being taught to drive. Michael might have been a good driver, but he was a rotten instructor (sometimes.)

Before we even moved off, I had to sit through a lengthy lecture on the fact that our Beetle was an old lady and had to be treated very, very gently. There was to be no excessive revving or stabbing at brakes or they could (and sometimes did) lock on. The Beetle treated us to a performance of this as we

embarked on a family holiday with Nana and the kids in the back. As we drove over the canal bridge by the Festival Inn, our stubborn old car decided she was going no further. Michael ended up lying underneath the car on his back, resplendent in orange Coal Board overalls, banging the offending brake cylinder with the ever-ready hammer. We hadn't even made it out of Trowell.

Oh, the amateur dramatics I would face during lessons. The muttered 'Oh God, my gearbox' or whatever if I hadn't pushed the left side pedal down enough. The sucking of air sharply through his teeth, the soft groan as he let his head slump against his window, the stupid whimpering noises he would make when we sailed past parked cars with, frankly, inches to spare.

'Get your backside into the middle of your lane!' he'd yell. It all made me very nervous to the point that one day as we were ending a lesson and nearly home, I turned a corner in fourth gear. The car started juddering and jumping as I put the brake on to slow it down. My husband's anguished groan pushed me over the edge. I yanked on the handbrake, stopping the car (it had stalled anyway.) In the middle of the road, I got out, slammed the door and stalked off, leaving him sitting there. I furiously strode away vowing never to get in a car with him again.

Of course, after a prolonged 'quiet period', I did and eventually I got the hang of things and our dear car's quirks. I used to drive us to Ilkeston to go to work every evening and Michael and Trisha, our daughter, were waiting for me at the end of my shift to drive home. So, I had regular lessons with fewer but sometimes still anguished dramatics.

I put in for my test and failed but no matter. I put in for a second test soon after. I was very nervous although Michael had taken me round and round the test circuit until I knew every little bump.

The examiner looked a little bemused when telling me to move off from the test centre. I pushed my arm between us and fumbled around looking for the starter button and the engine suddenly burst into life with that unmistakable Beetle roar. Upon our return we did the Highway Code bit, and I was amazed to be told I'd passed. I had to open the door for him to get out… it tended to stick a bit and he seemed to be struggling.

I was now no longer tethered to Awsworth. I was free for the first time in years and was soon nipping here, there and everywhere. Well, to Ilkeston and back; to work, the shops and nipping to my Mam and dad's was my limit actually. Michael used to say I was like a tram on a fixed track. I wasn't very confident out of my patch so when Michael started making casual remarks about me returning to my 'proper line of work', as he put it, I ignored him. A little later I read in the Nottingham Evening Post that due to former education cuts there was now a shortage of teachers in Nottinghamshire. Nottingham Trent University were starting refresher course for teachers who had taken a break from the profession and would like to return. I had, by this time, lost all my confidence and had given up any thoughts of returning to the profession that I had loved.

'Forget it!' I thought. 'I'm dreaming. I won't be applying.'

A couple of days later an application pack and course content popped through our letterbox.

'Nothing to do with me,' Michael protested, 'they must have you on a list.'

'Don't lie!' I replied. 'You want putting on a list!'

I finally gave in and reluctantly filled out the forms. To my dismay I was invited down for an interview and was driven there by Michael. I was accepted on to the course. 'I can't go. How can I drive all that way?' 'What?!' he replied 'It's only the other side of Queens Medical Centre. Don't worry we'll do some trial runs.'

I think if it had been necessary, he would have carried me there on his back, barefoot, over broken glass.

We did a few trial runs until I knew the way. He changed his shifts to nights and every morning we would grimly set off into rush hour in the Beetle with his bike in the back, the front wheel sticking out between us in the front seats.

Once he had got me to the Clifton campus and I was safely deposited in the building, he would cycle back home to Awsworth. Getting back home, though, was my problem and for the first few runs I would arrive home exhausted. He was right, as usual, but my confidence grew. The course was intensive and hard work but the tutors and other ladies on the course (who had all taken career breaks for similar reasons) were lovely. We all had the same self-doubts but quickly got back into picking up our old skills and getting up to speed with any new changes that had occurred.

I finished the course and had to apply for a job with Notts County Council but first I had to go for a medical. This took place at a surgery the other side of Trent Bridge. Needless to say, in those pre satnav days we had a trial run with Michael saying, 'just keep in the inside lane going over Trent Bridge and you will go straight to the surgery, you can't go wrong. Only an idiot could get lost going over Trent Bridge.'

Yes, well he didn't consider bullies who wouldn't let me into the inside lane in my banger and instead I just had to keep going and going.

Eventually I found myself sitting outside Wilford Hill Crematorium. I finally managed to navigate my way back, pointing the Beetle towards Nottingham and, to my amazement, arrived somewhat late for my appointment, outside the surgery. I had made it. Like the intrepid explorers who had fearlessly gone before me.

'Your blood pressure's a little high, Mrs O'Neill,' the doctor said. 'No surprise there,' I thought.

I was accepted by Nottingham County Council as a supply teacher and started my new job immediately, returning to a life that I had thought gone forever.

I had a very obliging supply organiser who, because of my anxiety over getting lost and being late, would send me more and more to Manning Girls' School in Aspley. Just by the driving test centre!

After a few weeks, the Deputy Head popped her head into my classroom and said, 'Betty, the Head would like to see you at break please.'

Well, whichever side of the fence you are on in school, being summoned suddenly to the Head's office does not usually end well so my glass was more than half empty as I apprehensively knocked on her door. It needn't have been. It was tea and biscuits and the offer of a permanent part-time art post. She then put the icing on the cake adding, 'I wondered, Betty, if you would consider becoming the school's permanent supply teacher? I'm afraid it will mean you are in all day, every day.'

Would I?! I had gone in expecting 'the sack' and come out with two jobs! Manning Girls became the third school in my career and was just as lovely as the first two I'd worked in. I loved every minute I was there. I had been so lucky. The driving lessons in our beloved Beetle had paid off.

CHAPTER 48

On the Buses

I have, on occasion, spoken of the characters in our rather insular communi-ty in the years after the war. Many of these had sprung from the number of young men who had been in the armed forces together. Some had been away from home for six long years between 1939-45 living, in many cases, dangerous and (dare I say it) exciting times for a few. They had done in the armed forces what, in those days, was unheard of for ordinary working-class people - travelled all over the world, albeit in dangerous circumstances.

Returning to civilian life or 'Civvy Street', many of these young men found it difficult to come to terms with the humdrum nature of a normal job. A good few of these men found their way to working on our transport system such as the railways, public transport, haulage or, perhaps, with the Royal Mail. They found this type of work less restrictive, and it gave them a much greater freedom than factory or office jobs. Many of the transport companies then were loosely based on the orderly military style discipline they had become used to. The train, bus, and post office employees would all wear quasi-military style uniforms.

We had four different bus companies operating in and around Ilkeston. There was the Midland General Omnibus Company, a very large organisation that operated as far as Mansfield; Trent, which was based in Derby; Barton and Felix. Just about everyone used public transport during this period when cars were either not available or affordable to the wider population in the way they are today. The buses were always full at peak times and remained busy throughout the day.

All the buses had crews and most of the regular travelling public knew them by their name or perhaps their derogatory nickname. There were no 'one man' operated buses as we have today. Everyone, of course, knew the conductors or 'duckies' as they were called - more so than the drivers who drove the bus from his separate cab. There were the miserable, always

grumpy ones and the comedians, who would often have the whole bus in an uproar with their never-ending banter, jokes and quips. The bus was their stage, and it was a pleasure to travel, and you would often get off with a smile on your face.

There were the crafty ones who would sometimes, when given the fare, press half of it back in your hand and move on without issuing a ticket. At peak times on the Ilkeston town service route with short stages they would pack so many passengers onto the bus, they couldn't get around to collect the fares. The ducky would have to stand on the platform, reeling off the tickets as the passengers got off, making sure that very few got past him without paying. The handle on his ticket machine would flash like lightning and a long roll of issued tickets would hang from it with who knows what fare printed on it.

It was an altogether different story should an oncoming bus signal that there was an inspector waiting up ahead. No matter how crowded the bus was, the ducky would be through the standing crowd like a rat up a drainpipe, issuing tickets left, right and centre, shouting loudly, 'fares please,' as the inspector got on.

One very well-known character who lived on Station Road and drove buses in Ilkeston was Mr Elton, known to one and all as 'Rocky'. Rocky drove his bus like a racing car, much to the delight of all the children and was tolerated by most of the adults. Kids would hop from foot to foot with glee when they saw who was driving the bus as it approached their stop. They would whoop with delight as he went over the Gallows Inn Bridge at the bottom of Nottingham Road at high speed. The bridge seemed much steeper then as a child and your bottom would sometimes leave the seat to cheers from some of your fellow passengers.

Rocky was rumoured among the children to have been a sergeant major during the war and he growled at everyone good naturedly, especially colleagues, as if he was still one. He was a short, stocky, handsome Italian looking man who had black wavy hair when younger. He never married and stayed in his lodgings on Station Road for the rest of his life. He called his elderly landlady Ma, and he thought the world of her. He always carried a small case to work with him, holding a flannel, towel, soap and a clean shirt which he changed into, halfway through shift on his break at the depot (where Tesco now stands). He seemed to be a little obsessive about his appearance which was perhaps a result of his army service.

On Christmas Day a skeleton service ran from Ilkeston to Nottingham every hour or so, just for part of the day. I was told Rocky always volunteered for this duty. He would be driving along deserted roads with few passengers.

Very little moved on Christmas Day then and I always thought it a little sad that he had nothing else to do at such a special time.

Sometimes, at around 4.30am, when on an early shift, he would go from the top of Station Road down to Chaucer Street to walk with my brother-in-law's elder sister (who was a young ducky then) if she was starting her shift at a similar time. He would see her safely to the depot that was then on Park Road, a good walk on cold dark mornings. Rocky was always the perfect gentleman.

He got into the habit when driving his B2 or C6 to Nottingham early in the morning of stopping in the middle of the stretch of road alongside Trowell Moor to feed the horses. They would come galloping to the hedge when they saw the blue double decker pull up, much to the amusement of some but the irritation of other passengers who had to catch connections and who sometimes missed them. He was reported and warned again and again by management. Inspectors would be waiting for his arrival in Nottingham after such complaints and he was given a verbal and then a final written warning. Rocky though was a law unto himself and carried on doing his thing.

Inevitably he was summoned to head office at Langley Mill and sacked. Such was the outcry over this popular driver's ousting that a petition was started by the travelling public of Ilkeston for his reinstatement. Can you imagine that happening today?! Rocky was duly asked to return to Langley Mill, and, on appeal, his dismissal was changed - mainly because of the petition - to a week's suspension with a warning that he had to change his ways. A thoroughly chastened Rocky assured the traffic manager that there would be no more interrupted journeys.

Rocky was Rocky though and, in those days, still a hot-headed young man. Before long he was driving like a bat out of hell again! One day he was coming up Station Road rather too fast and he hit the large green junction box on the pavement which was about five feet high and three or four feet long. This controlled the traffic lights onto Bath Street. He didn't just clip it - he flattened it, severely damaging the front of his bus at the same time. Chaos ensued for a while until it was replaced with the police having to control traffic throughout the day. He was sacked the same day with no right of appeal.

Rocky soon found work with the Co-op as a coal bagger. It was the worst job imaginable for such a fastidious man. The 1cwt weight coal bags that he had to carry on his back from the side of the lorry were about half his size and he was often seen looking a little worse for wear as he staggered along with a large coal bag on his back, a cloth covering the back of his head and shoulders. Covered in coal dust, he was not amused as ex colleagues passed by pipping the horns of their buses. Rocky loved his buses and would go down to Langley Mill at least once a week begging for his job back. Such was his popularity the management eventually relented and allowed him back with the warning that this was it - his very last chance.

My husband trained as a driver with Midland General when he was twenty-two and halfway through the training course it was found that he had made a mistake with his age. It was company policy that drivers should not be employed under twenty-three. At first, he was told he couldn't continue to be employed because of this. His story still remains that he was such a fantastic driver (realms of fantasy I think) they allowed him to stay on. In doing so he would have to stay on the short route 'town service' from Hallam Fields to Cotmanhay until he was twenty-three. He agreed but within a few days the novelty of driving a double decker backwards and forwards to Cotmanhay had worn off…

One Saturday morning when an inspector stopped his bus at the Rutland Hotel and told him a driver had been taken ill and would he like to take a coach to Blackpool, he replied 'Oh yes please!' The thought of driving a nice coach to the coast instead of his rickety old double decker all day was very appealing. He followed the inspector to Brussells Terrace where two coaches

stood, and a red-faced Rocky was busy loading the last of the
luggage for over a hundred people onto both of them. Reality kicked in then
and he had to admit to the inspector that he hadn't got the faintest idea how
to get to Blackpool.

'Well, you've got a route written down for you.'

'I can't drive and read that, can I?' he said.

So Rocky was brought over and the situation explained. Rocky was groaning,
holding his hands to his head, and doing a lot of 'I don't believe this', but in
the end agreed to be Michael's mentor and guide him all the way there. He
then boarded the bus and loudly told the passengers, who were all familiar
with Rocky, of course, 'This lad's new. Just passed his PSV driving test. He
doesn't know his way to Blackpool, and he's never driven one of these buses
before, so good luck!'

With that he marched off saying, 'and don't run into the back of me.'

Silence on the bus.

'Right, thanks for that Rocky,' Michael replied.

Michael said later that he never again had so many back seat drivers as on
that journey to Blackpool! Rocky, though, was as good as gold and took his
time but his joke backfired a little when Michael's collection was presented,
along with a round of applause (and no doubt a sense of relief as the
passengers arrived safely in Blackpool. It equalled his weekly wage, much to
Rocky's disgust. Rocky said he should split it seeing as he had loaded the
luggage. Michael was pretty green, but not so green that he would part with
half of his collection.

Drivers' hours were not so strictly enforced in the sixties and my husband
would often work a double shift on his day off if he could. It was quite
normal to see a driver asleep in a chair with a coat over him catching forty
winks in the canteen on his break at the depot. Discipline was pretty strict
though and running early, or missing runs was a sackable offence.

One hot summer two drivers, who had been warned for not wearing their neckties, were sacked. So my husband, who had been napping on his break, awoke in a panic after discovering his tie was missing. After unsuccessfully searching for it he had to take over a bus, worrying all the time that he would be jumped by an inspector. A little later he was alarmed to see a bus travelling in the opposite direction with his yellow necktie tied to the radiator cap. There it was resplendent on the front of the bus, flapping merrily in the wind. For the rest of his shift, he passed this bus every hour or so going in the opposite direction.

A lot of this pranking and fooling around came usually from the older ex-soldiers. When he came home and told me this tale I was not amused. We had a large mortgage, our first baby on the way and only his wage coming in. His cry of 'it wasn't my fault!' cut no ice with me. I had heard that excuse too many times to know that he was probably involved somewhere along the way. I told him, in no uncertain terms, that if he came home with his cards through such tomfoolery at work his tie wouldn't be swinging in the wind alone on the front of the next double decker going to Nottingham.

Michael said that it was a privilege to work with some of those men. I met a few at their sports and social events and children's Christmas parties. There was one driver, a giant of a man, who was the drill instructor during the war for paratroopers at Haddon Hall. He worked alongside his two, not-quite-so large sisters who were duckies and always seemed to be laughing or joking. Ex-marine commandos, bomb disposal experts, desert rats - so many men from across the forces all still up for a laugh, comradeship and a bit of devilment.

You would sometimes see some of these men years later when they had retired in the run up to Remembrance Day selling poppies in the Albion Centre or outside of the Co-op with a chest full of gleaming medals. You would wonder what stories they could tell, but few did. The horrors of war and those terrible times remained locked away.

Michael enjoyed his time working for Midland General, until the day he left (suddenly, but intact!). He had never had so many friends nor has had since. He popped in to see Rocky a couple of weeks before he died and remarked how sad it was to see this once strong, cocky man so diminished by age.

They had a laugh and a chat (about buses!).

Rocky recalled that first time they met. 'You didn't know your apex from your elbow did you, Mike?' (well, something like that anyway). What a great guy and a true gentleman he was. R.I.P Rocky. Rock on!

CHAPTER 49

Cossall Pit:
A Miner's Tale

Our dad, like many men around us, was a miner. He worked at Cossall Pit, where the Cossall Industrial Estate now stands. The large hill that stands behind the industrial estate is the old spoil tip where all the waste that came out of the mine was dumped - much of it smoking and burning underground for many years. The area on the opposite side of the viaduct bridge alongside the canal where a brickworks once stood was also smoking and the ground hot, the fire eventually burning its way beneath the canal. Children were warned that the ground could collapse under them if they played on it. The large hill was eventually transformed into a ski slope long after the mine closed and enjoyed brief success before going out of business.

Cossall Colliery was a drift mine, locally called a footrill (I'm told) - a mine which men walked into rather than the usual type where they were lowered down in a cage. Mining was very dangerous in the forties and fifties.

You would sometimes hear your parents or other children at school discussing some miner at the pit who lived on their street or nearby who had been killed or 'trapped' as they used to say with the loss of a limb or a broken back. I would then worry about my dad but after a few days when nothing bad had happened I would put it out of my mind, as children tend to do.

The miners used to walk home in all their muck and dirt, their helmets and knee pads still on and their 'snap tins' in their hands. My dad once went to work with a large jam pasty. He couldn't get into his snap tin so decided to just carry it inside his shirt with nothing around it. One of his friends was fooling about just before they went down and playfully punched him in his stomach, splattering the sticky jam all over the hairs on his chest, which must have been a shock for both parties!

Miners would bathe at home in front of the fire in a tin bath. There were no bathrooms in the terraced houses in most streets so when showers were installed at Cossall, the men thought they had the best jobs in the world.

One day my dad got his hand trapped while down the pit and his finger severed. The accident obviously caused him to bleed badly but he still insisted on having his shower before going to hospital.

Dad had to finish work at the age of fifty, like many other miners who were gasping for breath with diseased lungs. He had to go before many medical boards where he had to jump through hoops to get his sick pay. He found it a humiliating experience, faced with men who could (and did) talk rings around him, leaving him feeling hurt and angry. When told he had to go to Sheffield for x-ray investigations, he said he was too poorly and wouldn't go and that it would be a waste of time anyway. We nagged him into going, saying he would be a fool not to and that he would receive the compensation he deserved for the loss of his wages when they saw the state of his lungs. Eventually he relented and went, returning home in the evening completely exhausted after a long day. The results eventually came back saying that they

had found he was suffering from severe emphysema that was not work related. 'What did I tell you', Dad said. 'I know them, a complete waste of time.'

He was often very poorly, and one night around 1966 he collapsed at home and was rushed to Ilkeston Hospital coughing blood. He was then transferred to Newstead Hospital, a sanatorium where many sick miners went.

The Saturday after he was admitted, my sister and I set off to visit him, leaving my brother-in-law looking after my sister and his new baby. We caught a Midland General bus to Mansfield from the Rutland Hotel at the bottom of Bath Street and had to get off at the Newstead crossroads to catch another bus that went past the hospital. Having asked at a nearby shop when the next bus to the hospital or Newstead was, we were informed we had just missed it and there wouldn't be another for at least an hour (if it came at all), it being a private company that ran the service. Time was getting on, so we decided to walk.

Newstead Hospital was set in its own grounds in the middle of nowhere, so it was rather foolhardy for two young woman in heels, laden with fruit and other foods, to start walking. We set off down a narrow country road with hedgerows either side and no pavement and we walked and walked and walked. I've no idea of the distance but suffice to say it was a long way. Eventually we arrived, just as all the visitors were leaving and boarding the bus waiting outside! I said to my sister, 'we are going in. We have not come all this way for nothing. If anyone says anything just say we are nurses starting work.'

We marched boldly in, only to be stopped almost immediately by a Sister telling us that visiting was over and we would have to leave. There was no point in arguing as she clearly knew everyone who worked there and we were both starting to look a little worse for wear after our trek anyway. So we told her our sorry tale, replete with a tear or two shed by my accompanying drama queen, and she allowed us to go in to see him. 'Ten minutes and no more,' she said.

Dad was in a sort of large cubicle which held just four men.

Unfortunately, two had died overnight so the atmosphere was heavy. Dad was poorly but glad to see us. 'Where have you been?' he said, 'visiting's over.' We busily packed all the food and fruit we had bought into his locker.

'Oh, thank God!' he said, 'the food here is awful but is supposed to do us good.'

In no time at all we had to turn around and leave, only to find that the bus had long gone and with no prospect of another coming, now that visiting had ended for the day. It was autumn and starting to get dark but there was no option other than to start back up that long dark road, my sister squealing (and swearing) whenever the odd car came past seemingly skimming us by inches and putting us in fear of getting knocked down on the unlit road. Luckily, they were few and far between on that lonely road.

I said to Cynthia, 'come on let's get a move on or we're going to get run over.' As a young woman I was quite tall, but my sister is barely five feet nothing. We had to walk in single file, the road being so narrow and within minutes she started wailing, 'wait for me, Bett, you're going too fast!'

I had a feeling of déjà-vu, all she had to say now was 'I'll tell me mam if you don't wait' and I would have been transported back to our childhood. But she didn't… she went one better. 'Bett, I want a wee!' she shouted. 'You've got to wait!' Not long having had a baby, her bladder was a little unreliable.

We arrived at a gate which opened into a field and by this time it was practically dark. I shoved her through the gate muttering, 'get behind that hedge and hurry up!' 'Well, 'keep conk' and don't leave me,' she replied. Keep conk?! There was no one around for miles. She appeared after a few minutes in a relieved state saying, 'oh crikey that's better!' Which made me want to go. 'I've got to go,' I said. 'Keep a look out.' 'Well, dab in!' came the ungracious answer.

When I came out, she was gone, she was about a hundred yards up the road, her short legs going as fast as they could. 'Well, thanks a lot!' I shouted. 'I needed a bit of a start,' she shouted back. 'You go too fast!'

We eventually made the crossroads and after another long wait in the dark we caught the bus back to Ilkeston. It was very late when we arrived home and Mam was in the yard looking over the wall, up and down the street, convinced something had happened to either dad or us.

We have never forgotten that journey. We were both utterly exhausted when we eventually got home, mainly from stress, I think. The doctors and nurses at the Newstead Hospital were fantastic at helping the miners. They were very caring but there was no way of curing their diseased lungs. Dad, like many of his workmates, died slowly and miserably over the years, eventually succumbing in 1985 - just four months after Mam had died.

Dad wasn't a special case. There were many like him in all mining communities across the country. The Coal Board would not admit that many miners were suffering from dust-related illnesses and refused them compensation, until (in lots of cases) long after they had died and for many former miners - not at all.

Eventually the unions did take up the miners' cases. I can't remember now what caused the change of heart or policy, but the Coal Board suddenly agreed to review cases if enough evidence was produced. This was years after many men had died and their next of kin couldn't get the evidence, records having been lost or destroyed by doctors and hospitals, being kept for only a finite number of years.

Few of the deceased men or their families got compensation for the illnesses suffered or their inability to work and it proved to be a shameful period in the country's mining history and the National Coal Board.

CHAPTER 50

The Fire

Life's Little Ups and Downs

Our new baby girl was joyfully welcomed into the world on a fine New Year's Day afternoon. My husband, at the moment of birth, decided he badly needed a sandwich and departed quickly, returning much later when everything was done and dusted. 'Oh, sorry, have I missed it?' he said, contritely.

She was perfect in every way. That is apart from one minor inconvenience that was to give the whole family hell for the next four years! She had a huge separation issue from the moment she was born. I think she would have been quite content staying where she was: nicely warm and comfy, instead of being dragged into the world.

She couldn't bear to be away from close contact with me, for even the shortest of times, before turning into a squalling bundle of fury that went on and on until you would fear for her health. Even in the maternity ward she would soon be taken from her cot at the end of the bed by a nurse and put into my arms where she would instantly settle down and sleep. Most new parents go through sleepless nights with new additions to the family, our little problem lasted until she went to nursery school! It went on, day after day, night after night. I would lay her in her cot at night and creep out of her room as soon as she fell asleep, her plastic wind-up music box softly tinkling 'Raindrops keep falling on your head' (Oh, how I came to hate that tune!)

Within half an hour or so she would wake to find me gone and would go absolutely berserk. I would jump out of bed and race back into her room to soothe her, trying (and failing) to make sure Michael, who had to be up early for work, got something like a reasonable night's rest. The doctor wanted to give baby some medication to make sure she gave me a break, but I was definitely not going to allow that. So he tried me on anti-depressants which just turned me into a shambling automaton.

It's no exaggeration to say the situation nearly broke the three of us. We were getting reports from school saying our son was always tired. I would clean and cook with her on my hip. I couldn't put her down for even a short time and it certainly wasn't through lack of trying. There was a baby food scare on at the time with some sudden cot deaths and we were told that we had to feed her National Dried Milk which she didn't like and so she was never content after her bottle which didn't help our situation. We never started a meal without her erupting with fury.

I was always desperately tired and depressed. Christmas was approaching at the end of that first year and I was trying to get everything organised for the next day. My mother-in-law was coming to stay over Christmas, which I hoped would give me a little respite. I sometimes despaired, though, at how many toys we already had in the house - cars with no wheels, broken bits and bobs with parts missing that you were not allowed to throw away and an abundance of things for the new baby that she was too young to play with. We had very generous parents - too generous! The children's aunts and grandparents were always kindly buying them gifts and there would be lots more tomorrow after Santa had been. So, on this particular Christmas Eve afternoon I was at the end of my tether through lack of sleep. I was, as usual, dead on my feet. I picked up a plastic toy that was broken and threw it on the fire in sheer frustration and exasperation. 'More coming in the morning', I moaned… and then watched in horror as the thing burst into a ball of flames and disappeared up the chimney.

'Oh, oh, Michael! Michael!' I shouted. He came rushing in and looked in horror at the fiercely burning plastic that was dripping from up the chimney down into the grate. We were both on our knees peering up the chimney but could see nothing but a few seconds later we heard plenty. A deep, frightening roar came from up above, getting louder and louder. It soon sounded like an express train. All this from one small (ish) toy! I grabbed the baby and ran outside. I'd never been so terrified in my life. A column of flame was shooting from the chimney pot, neighbours were coming out to watch and give advice. Thick, black, evil smelling smoke rolled down the street. I ran up my neighbour's path, into her house and stood with her,

watching through her living room window at the frenzied antics of Michael, who kept running in and out of the house looking up at the flames coming from the top of our chimney and then running back in (to do what I don't know.)

Later he told me he had been lying on his back squirting water up the chimney from a squeezy bottle. The chimney pot was a long narrow pot, taller than normal that cracked from top to bottom with the heat and stayed cracked for the next twenty years before I had it replaced by a builder while Michael was at work, mainly because he had intended to do it himself to save a bob or two.

The Fire Brigade were called and duly arrived, our baby happily on my hip interestedly watching all the activity on the street. 'Christmas Eve!' I thought. Mother-in-law arriving the next day for Christmas. This was all I needed. I felt wretched and thanked God Michael was home from work. My neighbour, baby and I watched from her front window as firemen crawled over our roof and squirted water down our chimney. Our TV aerial was pulled off the stack and lay on the roof. 'That's Christmas definitely ruined now,' I thought. Michael stood with a group of firemen talking animatedly and pointing at me standing at the window.

One of the firemen with a white helmet with stripes on it, who I took to be in charge, turned and with a smile on his face shook his fist at me. 'Oh, thank you for that, Michael,' I thought, 'thank you very, very much, you tell-tale tit. You couldn't wait to blame me, could you?' Giving him my death stare, I thought vengefully, 'you'll pay for that mate. Santa's leaving nothing for you tomorrow!' OK it was my fault, but he could have taken the blame for me like a good husband. The firemen were lovely and very understanding having given Michael a friendly lecture on the dangers of throwing plastic on a fire. They even fixed the TV aerial back on to the stack.

The fireplace and house took a bit of cleaning up and we had an awful smell in all the rooms for days later. Christmas was saved, though the fire wasn't mentioned. We laughed about it later (much later.) It wasn't to be my only run in with our chimney though, although the next time I was blameless…

As Dickens famously wrote, 'It was the best of times. It was the worst of times.'

CHAPTER 51

The Chimney Sweep

Life's Little Ups and Downs

Michael worked at the time for the NCB (National Coal Board). We had a lot of coal to burn since Michael's allowance was a tonne every five weeks and so the fire was in 24/7. The chimney had to be swept regularly, yes, my job, 'because you're good at it!'

With a Fine Fare plastic bag wrapped around my head, blankets covering the fireplace to stop soot fall coming into the room and a sock in the middle to push the rods through after fitting the brush in the chimney opening, I did the chimney at least twice a year. My dad had given us the rods, and I think they had been his dad's possibly, my grandad's. They were about a hundred years old then, bent out of shape from being forced up awkward chimneys. I had complained about them for a long time, but all Michael would say was (and still is saying) 'there's miles left in them, nothing wrong with them' and 'rods don't grow on trees.'

So, on this particular day he sat on the dust-cover covering the chair, watching me and I was getting comments like 'That bag on your head really suits you, you should have had one years ago.'

Not for the first time he came up with another brilliant idea for me to get back to work. 'You know,' he said, 'there is only one chimney sweep in Awsworth. You could have your own little business. You're really good at it'. 'Oh yes,' I said 'will we be buying a van then for me to get about in, with all my gear?'

'No,' he replied, 'no need for that, you would only work in Awsworth in your spare time. I'll make you a barrow!' I said, 'dream on if you think I'm pushing a barrow around Awsworth, especially one that you've made'. 'Ahh' he said, 'pride cometh before a fall. Too good to do that kind of work now, are we? Gone up in the world a bit, have we?' (smiling but having a little dig.) I didn't know how he dare say that, with me on my knees in the Co-op butchery scrubbing the floor every evening. It was at this point I was sweeping away, pushing and pulling at my rods. I was feeling a little resistance. Pulling the rods right out I said, 'The brush has come off.'

'WHAT?!' he shouted, jumping up from his chair. 'You've been twisting the rods the wrong way and you've unscrewed it.'

'No, I haven't,' I yelled, 'It's these rods, they are worn out - the threads are all worn where you screw one rod to the other and you know it, it's your own fault for being too tight to buy new rods.'

Suddenly, Michael's the expert, 'Don't worry I've got an old brush with only half its bristles left on in the shed, we'll push the lost one out.' So, this brush was duly screwed to the rods and pushed up the chimney with (thankfully) Michael now in charge. He pushed up as far as the rods would go and vigorously worked them up and down. He pulled them back down to find that that brush was missing too. Not to be beat he went to a neighbour and borrowed his brush. This was screwed into the rods regardless of me saying that the threads were no good and worn out. No, no, he knew best.

'I'll cross thread it so it can't come off.' Shoving the brush up, he found the blockage rammed and, pushing violently, pulled the rods back down to find that our neighbours brush was gone too. So now we had three brushes up the chimney. 'Okay, don't panic' says the expert, 'I've got something to sort this out.' He went outside to the back of the shed where he had a seven-foot hollow, aluminium tube (something else he had acquired that you never knew when it might come in handy) with a bigger bore than our rods. Where he'd got it from, I knew not! He bent the top foot or so down, to make something like a shepherd's crook, it was hollow, and the rods fitted snugly inside. We wrapped around the join with masking tape to really secure it. 'Do you want to do it?' he asked. 'Oh no,' I said 'not likely, you do it. You aren't blaming me for this mess we are in'.

He shoved this giant hook up the chimney and after some wriggling and easing he latched on. 'Got it' he said triumphantly and started pulling. 'Crikey, they are really jammed' pulling with all his might the rods suddenly came down with a rush and to his dismay the hook was missing too. I daren't say a word. I wasn't used to hearing him use that sort of language. We cleaned up and Michael said he would go to the fire station for advice. On going outside, he found the aluminium hook he had made, lying in the front garden attached firmly to the TV aerial.

There was no sign of the three brushes. He went to the fire station and was advised by a fireman who was trying to keep a straight face to take a chance and light a fire.

We followed his advice, lit the fire and nothing happened for some time. Then, weeks later as we sat in front of the fire watching TV, one dark evening there was a rumble and a rattle, and all the metal bits and charred wood came tumbling down the chimney in a cloud of soot. We had quite a bit of cleaning up to do. The house had a horrible smell of soot that lasted for days but at last we could stop worrying about the chimney catching fire. Our neighbour never did get his brush replaced, being told it was on its last legs anyway and we'd done him a favour by getting rid of it.

I never did get any new brushes. After that we had the professionals come and do the job and Michael never mentioned me starting a chimney sweeping business again.

CHAPTER 52

Beetling along on Holiday

Life's Little Ups and Downs

The VW Beetle that we owned in the eighties was a parochial (not liking to leave Ilkeston and its surrounding areas) and temperamental thing. It was certainly a love-hate relationship between us. Going away on holiday, however, would raise tensions to a whole new and critical level.

My parents-in-law would take my husband, Michael, on holiday every year as a child and she was determined this family tradition would continue with our children after Michael's dad had died. So off we would go on caravanning holidays, and you could bet your cotton socks on some crisis arising, without fail.

His mum once had a bad asthma attack in the middle of the night on the first night of the holiday and lay gasping for breath all night, which coincided with our son's temperature becoming dangerously high from a bug he had gone down with, and he spent the night clinging to me crying.

Rain was thundering down on the caravan roof and at first light on that Sunday morning, Michael was out trying to find a doctor and to get antibiotics if he could find a chemist open. We were all exhausted before we had really started the holiday.

After that summer he declared, 'we are going upmarket this year! Forget about caravanning, we're going to a holiday camp with plenty for the kids to do.'

'Ooh!' I thought. 'Butlins.' Well, not quite… it was a little camp outside Skegness with chalets, a Baltic swimming pool (which would see off the most hardened Channel swimmer) a field and a clubhouse. That was about it - but the price was right!

As usual, the rain was pouring down and a howling gale blew. The skies were menacing but regardless, we all had to put on our rainwear and go out and sit in a little concrete shelter looking out at a very bleak, wild and windy North Sea, its waves crashing fiercely against the sea wall. My mother-in-law, the children's much loved 'Nana' was old school.

'You are on holiday, you will enjoy it, whatever the weather,' was her mantra - regardless of sand getting everywhere it could possibly get. If the obligatory sandwiches and flask accompanied us, it would be fine.

Feeling pretty exhausted on the first night, we had our evening meal and decided on an early bedtime. We awoke the next morning to find we were ankle deep in floodwater, our chalet enjoying a 'premium location' in the dip. After moving to another chalet, we seemed to spend the rest of the day drying stuff out.

Keen to get the most out of our swanky resort's entertainment programme, my young daughter was desperate to enter the fancy dress competition. With most of our stuff soggy and it probably not being the best option to send her as a drowned rat, we decided to improvise. Her raincoat was duly covered in scarlet balloons from the shop and behold she went as the song by Nena '99 Red Balloons'. She lost to Miss Muffet. I swore there was some jiggery pokery going on with the winner's mother and one of the judges, whom she seemed to be very friendly with. Our daughter was obviously the best by far, plus the fact that I'd nearly done myself an injury spending the morning blowing up all those balloons meant we felt worthy of some recognition!

The driving rain continued for most of the week, and I was glad to get home to a warm fire. The car behaved and ran, as my husband kept saying, 'like a sewing machine.' He decided with this in mind that it was time to explore further afield and booked our upmarket Butlin's holiday to Somerset. Nana immediately declared the car would never make it. 'Don't be silly,' Michael replied. 'It's got a new (reconditioned) engine. It's running like a sewing machine' (his current favourite phrase.) We were all worried and doubtful but of course he knew best. With the roof rack piled high with everything but the kitchen sink, off we set. Michael was right, our little Beetle was behaving for once. Money well spent on that new engine.

She was purring like a pussy cat as she cruised along the motorway at a steady 65 mph with the five of us crammed in. Everyone finally started to relax and enjoy the ride. It was short lived. We nearly made it to Bristol when there was a terrific bang and clouds of blue and black smoke started to pour

out behind us. Having spluttered to a halt in an emergency vehicle hard standing, the Beetle made a final death rattle and immediately expired. 'Okay, don't worry!' he said. 'We'll get the AA out, they'll soon sort it'.

The AA eventually arrived a couple of hours later, 'Oh!' the AA man said, shaking his head. 'I can't do anything with that I'll have to call Relay for you. You will have to decide where you want to go - on to your destination or back home. Where shall I tell base?'

'Minehead!' Michael said. 'Home!' chorused his mother and I. 'You're outvoted, Michael.'

'I'm not bothered!' he sulked, his lip coming out further and further. 'I'm going to Minehead with the car and you lot can go where you like. I've paid and I'm going, I'll fix the car when I get there.' That special family holiday feeling had certainly departed as we all silently stood, yards apart, waiting for Relay. Nana stood alone looking ready to explode, not speaking to me because I wouldn't (couldn't) make him see sense. I was seething because I'd known something like this would happen. Our son loyally stood with his dad while our daughter stood with me, clutching her cuddly toys. The car was dragged up onto the tow truck and we all clambered into the truck's cab. We all sat silently in the cab, looking sideways out of different windows. The driver clearly thought we were all mad, his jolly attempt at conversation quickly fizzling out. Onwards to Minehead, in a stony silence.

We went through the camp's gates, which the jolly security man opened for us. 'Oh, you made it!' he bellowed cheerfully. 'You've missed your dinner though.' I pushed down a strong desire to physically retaliate...! Just to put the top hat on it they had given us the wrong chalet and we were a bedroom short. Nana finally started speaking the following Wednesday.

Michael fetched the garage man out to look at the Beetle. Turns out exploding pistons and damaged cylinder heads are expensive, and holidaymakers ripe for plucking!

He shook his head and sucked his teeth. 'It will cost you about a thousand quid,' he said. 'WHAT?! No way! I'll scrap it first,' replied my evermore despairing husband (we hadn't got a thousand quid anyway.)

We walked despondently back to our chalet and then a minor miracle occurred. Right in the middle of the camp stood an RAC booth with a big sign: 'Join Now! Immediate Cover.' My husband stood gazing at it, his eyes wide with wonder and astonishment. I had another sinking feeling. 'No!' I said, grimly. 'Yes!' Michael replied, grinning. He is not one to look a gift horse in the mouth. 'It's a miracle!'

Off he scuttled to tell the RAC man his sad tale. 'Well!' said the RAC man, 'They probably think everyone's here under their own steam, so they are on safe ground saying immediate cover. There's nothing in the small print to stop you joining and calling us if it won't start and you're certainly far enough away from home. He signed up immediately and paid his dues. We were now in the AA and the RAC.

He met up with his Mum later, regaling that he'd fixed it. Oh, the relief on her face. He neglected to tell her just how he'd fixed it. When he eventually told her she would be going home in a lorry she stopped speaking to him again. So come Saturday morning the RAC was duly called and to our horror, amid clouds of blue smoke, he got it going again. 'Oh, nope!' Looks like it's something serious. I'll have to get Relay to you. Can I see your membership card? Oh! A new member too, I see.' He grinned at us all. 'Lucky you.'

I wanted the ground to swallow me up.

We went through the gates late that Saturday morning, the same cheery security man back on duty. 'Oh! This is a new one!' he bellowed, 'Arriving on the back of an AA wagon and departing on an RAC truck!' I was hoping for a swift death and started to worry that Nana was on her way, with the agonised look and groans emerging from her. It was a long journey back to Awsworth with neither of us talking to Michael or each other for the duration.

When we got home, I cooked our driver a large fry up and Michael literally filled the lorry cab with 56lb plastic bags of coal, of which we had tonnes stacked up the garden, courtesy of the National Coal Board, which we were frankly glad to get rid of. The driver was very grateful but rather worried he would get another breakdown call on his way back to Minehead, his cab full of cobbles and no room for passengers.

Years later Michael's aunt told him his mother had vowed never to go on another calamitous family holiday with us again. She did, of course, along with her flask. It was to be the next holiday we went on that turned out to be the final straw for her.

CHAPTER 53

A Tale of Two Pianos

Life's Little Ups and Downs

When we got married we were in the same position as many young couples, that is, we were pretty hard up most of time. With just one wage coming in things were pretty tight. When the new baby arrived, even with the generosity of both our parents, things got even tighter.

We had no TV, a second-hand cooker, a cheap three-piece suite, a kitchen table and four chairs - a wedding present from Michael's parents which we still have and wouldn't part with. There are too many happy memories around that table to replace it with something flash and we have no one to impress but we do treasure our memories.

Michael's Aunt May was throwing out her old radiogram. The record deck part of it was broken beyond repair. 'You can have it if it's any good to you,' she told Michael. 'The radio has a lovely tone.' He brought it home, sawed it in half and sawed the remaining two legs half off, leaving just the radio half standing lop-sided on two shortened legs, and a gaping open wound where once the other half had been. I wasn't impressed, but two bricks under one side levelled it up beautifully. It was placed in the alcove with the open wound down the side pushed up against the wall, completely hiding it from view. The rich sound coming from the radio inside the polished cabinet, topped with a nice vase of flowers impressed those who didn't know its history and couldn't see its injuries.

What we did have though, that very few other people of our ilk had, was Michael's Art Deco piano which his mother had been glad to wave goodbye to, freeing up the alcove in her house that it had occupied since Michael was six.

This piano wasn't any old upright antique, unlike the one that I had grown up with and had had to master. Mine had been made sometime in the 1800s with brass candlestick holders on either side of the front which could be moved from side to side for the candles placed in them to cast the best light on the music, with decorative scroll work on the front.

Michael's grandfather had bought his Art Deco piano in the early 1930s. His grandmother was quite a gifted pianist. We were told it was a Yacht Piano and only twenty of this particular type had been made. The keyboard folded up into the front of the piano and could be locked in place. It had a gleaming black ebony finish, with silver pedals; obviously an expensive, quality piano with a matching piano stool with a leather seat. The finish on it shone and reflected like a black mirror, no angular corners on it, all rounded tastefully. It wouldn't have been out of place in an expensive setting today. It really was a thing of beauty with gold lettering on the dashboard in front of the keys right in the middle above middle C which said, STURNE. It had a rich clear tone always having been tuned regularly. I think my old upright had 88 keys. Our Yacht piano had seven octaves as I remember, making it slightly smaller than my old one.

Both Michael and I had been sent for piano lessons from the ages of six to sixteen. I went to Grangers at Hallam Fields, Michael went to a teacher on Church Street, Cotmanhay. A boy walking through the Cotmanhay estate in the fifties, neatly dressed for his lesson carrying his leather music case could sometimes be a prime target. He recalled the time he arrived at his teacher's door with blood running down his cheeks onto his white shirt after a running, stone-throwing battle with some other boys who managed to score a bull's eye to his forehead. The piano teacher's wife cleaned him up and he was sent home as not fit for purpose. Michael thought it was all well worthwhile to escape his dreaded music theory being marked.

The time came when, like most youngsters nearing adulthood, I suppose he rebelled and refused to take any more lessons or to spend any more time on piano practise. Practise that had previously been every day, seven days a week for at least thirty minutes each day for all those years; all that imposed discipline went out of the window.

So, at first, the piano in our new small three bedroomed semi was a bit of a novelty. Neither of us would make concert pianists but we could still play after ten years of lessons and daily practise. We both read music fluently and could knock some nice tunes out (as long as the music wasn't too difficult). We would both play piano duet or piano with four hands together, if there was nothing worth listening to on our fancy radio, and we did get quite good at it. It was amusing, not by today's home entertainments though, I hasten to add. But you make do with what you've got, don't you?

They were happy days. As so often happens though, work and life got in the way of those early days. Long hours out at work with youngsters to care for soon put those early musical interludes to rest. The keyboard was folded up into the piano and locked (even the silver key was artistically designed) to stop annoying little fingers banging on the keys every five minutes, which combined with a constantly screaming child and lack of sleep could push you close to the edge sometimes.

The years rolled by quickly, the key disappeared, lost forever! The keyboard locked into the piano forever too it seemed. There it sat in our small living room, looming large and sometimes I thought it was laughing at me. Why couldn't we have a beautiful living room? How could we when this big, dark useless monstrosity now dominated the room? Then, out of the blue the problem was solved. Or so I thought. Michael was at work, as usual (he seemed to live there.) I had been given some magazines, Beautiful Homes and Country Life. As I flipped through I spotted a picture of an upmarket house with the patio doors wide open, three or four posh children standing with Daddy. He stood with his dogs sitting obediently alongside, his shotgun folded over the crook of his arm in front of the doors. Behind them, in their gorgeous drawing room, stood a piano. Not just any piano, it was like ours. But it was different!

It was a baby grand piano. Not only was it a grand piano, but it was also a white grand piano. That was my light bulb moment. I was going to have my beautiful living room. I didn't think it through. In a moment of madness, I made my mind up instantly. I went out to the shed, got a tin of white gloss paint and painted our piano and stool white, from top to bottom. (I think I must have had a brainstorm.) I must say, I was quite handy with a decorator's brush when I was young, and I made a good job of it and was pleased with the result. Our living room looked different now. It was no longer dominated by a big black monstrosity. Now, it was dominated by a big, white monstrosity!

I waited at first, expectantly. Then, after looking at it for a few hours, apprehensively, waiting for Michael to come home. Would he like it? Well, that was a big fat NO! 'OH MY GOD! WHAT HAVE YOU DONE?' He went very quiet and couldn't eat his dinner. Michael's father didn't speak to me for three months. Anyone would have thought I'd murdered his grandchild. We never did see his grandad for some time, and when we eventually did, he was somewhat offhand.

Some years later Michael decided the piano, which had now been moved to the kitchen, had to be unlocked. He went to see David Johnson who used to keep a hardware store on Station Road and after telling him the story, asked if he could help unlock it. 'No,' David said, 'however my friend, Charlie Moon, will be able to.' Charlie used to have a hardware/cafe shop at the upper end of Bath Street on the opposite side to the Smoothie Bar and a bit lower down. 'Charlie was a skilled locksmith when he was young,' David said, 'I'll get him to come round and have a look'.

Mr Moon came round one Sunday morning. He got out these little picks kept in a leather wallet. He inserted them into the keyhole, jiggled them about a little, and hey presto! Within a few minutes he had it open and the keyboard lowered for the first time in years. 'It wants tuning,' he said after playing a few notes. Mr Moon had it open in no time but stayed chatting for nearly two hours. He wouldn't take any payment. 'My pleasure, my dear,' he said 'and thank you for the tea and biscuits.' Such a nice gentleman!

We never did take up playing again. A little later Michael had not one of his greatest ideas. 'We'll move it upstairs,' he said. So, it was decided we would move it into our daughter's room, which was a large bedroom. I don't know what she thought of that idea, she was never asked!

How he got his elderly mother and myself to agree to help him I will never know. It was madness. The piano, from what I've read since, weighed in excess of 400lbs.

'Don't worry,' he said, 'we're not going to try to lift it - we couldn't, we will slide it up on decorators' planks, easy-peasy.'

'How do you think removal men do it? Trust me!' Hmmm.

The planks were set, and we managed to lever one end of the piano to the starting point on the plank at the bottom of the stairs, losing a shepherd's castor along the way. My washing line doubled as a rope ('I'm not an idiot,' says he!) was wrapped around the piano and then around Michael's waist as he stood above the piano with his mum and myself pushing from below. We actually got it moving. 'Oh,' I thought, 'perhaps he does know what he's talking about after all.'

Then things changed. The front of the piano was halfway up the stairs and suddenly we felt the weight. The piano seemed to want to slide back. Dora, Michael's mum, started wailing. 'We can't hold it, Michael, it's too heavy, I'll have to have a puff,' and sat down two stairs up leaving me to take the weight and hold it alone! She was asthmatic and had to have her inhaler if she got short of breath.

'Okay, don't stop pushing yet,' Michael shouted. 'Okay, yes, don't worry I've got it now, I've got it,' Michael shouted, taking all the weight on the rope. With the piano weighing over 400lbs and Michael weighing around 132lbs it was no contest.

We rebelled, refusing to try to take it up another inch. I could see both his mother and me being flattened, and Michael cut in half with the rope around his waist when the piano would have, without doubt, run back down. Our children left without parents or a nana! Michael was grumpy about faint hearted assistants and the piano was returned, after much effort, to the living room with the damaged castor now just propping up one corner.

Michael has always professed to being very handy with, well, anything that needed fixing (anything that involved paying a professional to fix anyway) and to be fair he would always give it a good go. I use the word handy very, very loosely here, but he did have a go.

'I'm taking whatever I can take off the piano to make it lighter, then we'll get it to the garage and I'll strip this awful paint off, restoring it to its former glory,' he said. With much effort and more muscular help from friends, this was eventually done. He tried paint stripper first, but the two coats of paint I'd put on were defeating his efforts and costing him dearly in expensive stripper.

That idea was abandoned, 'I'll warm it up and strip it off with a blowlamp,' he said. What could go wrong? Everything it seems. Fire, paint stripper, and paint on wood just don't mix. Part of the piano caught fire and it took ages to put out and was irreversibly damaged.

The piano was stripped down in a temper, cut up and put outside the gates for the dustbin men. Part of it, being used for firewood. That dashboard with the lovely gold lettering and the word STURNE is still in the garage, the veneer now peeling off, the once rich lettering now sadly faded. The milkman came through the gates and, seeing all the bits, had to open his mouth, 'Crikey are you really chucking this out?' That didn't improve Michael's mood. I kept out of the way!

When we had to clear my Mam and Dad's house after my dad died, the house clearance man looked at my old piano and said, 'Ah! An over-strung, under-damped German antique piano. It's in good condition.' (It ought to have been, the amount of polish that had been rubbed into it over the years.) 'A very nice cabinet. These are much sought after in America This could finish up crated up and shipped out.' Whether it was or not, I will never know. The price he gave us for it certainly didn't reflect his words. Who could have foreseen that scenario though? Our Yacht piano, now firewood; my old piano, perhaps now gracing a grand house in America.

Michael did suggest that I give it a quick coat of white gloss. He can be very sarcastic sometimes.

I can no longer read music, it's all Greek to me now. I went to bed one night and when I woke up, my life had changed forever. Speech and skills learned from childhood were pretty much all gone, along with life's worries, leaving a blank canvas. Strangely, most of my childhood memories, by some strange quirk of fate, were left where I could endlessly think about them in my quiet world. That is probably why I spend so much time thinking about the past. Strangely I was, and still am, happy. It was the start of a new kind of life.

A biblical phrase has often crossed my mind since that day.

The Lord giveth and the Lord taketh away.

CHAPTER 54

A Moment in Time

Throughout the country during the summer, a 1940s themed day or weekend often arises to remember that remarkable generation to whom we owe so much. Ilkeston Museum held their 1940s garden party on Saturday 29th June - which was very well attended. Many people took great effort to dress the part and the armed forces were portrayed by re-enactors in their WWII uniforms to remember the sacrifices made by thousands of our soldiers who died or were injured during the war and to commemorate the 75th anniversary of the D-Day landings.

Most of that generation who fought have now died but of all the men in our family who served and fought in the conflict, until recently we still had one with us. My uncle, Ken Holmes (our Dad's brother) was 99 at the time of

writing this article and served during the war on destroyers and frigates. One of the few left who fought throughout the war from beginning to end.

The local paper told his story in the 2017 November issue but since then, Ken has sadly died. However, during his lifetime he was awarded the Legion d'Honneur by France for his services during D-Day. The Legion of Honour is the highest French order of merit and was established in 1802 by Napoleon Bonaparte and retained by all later French governments and regimes.

Ken's destroyer, HMS Eskimo, was in battle alongside his flotilla against four German destroyers during the landings - two of which were sunk and two driven away badly damaged and on fire. Ken said his first ship, the Hurricane, which was torpedoed and had to be sunk was not a happy ship - the first lieutenant being a martinet. HMS Eskimo, a tribal class powerful destroyer, was both a happy ship and a lucky one. Sixteen tribal class destroyers were built for the Royal Navy and only four survived the war. Each ship had a complement of approximately two hundred men.

When told that he could probably have his medal awarded to him at the town hall by the mayor and a French dignitary with local TV coverage he shook his head and said, 'thanks, but no thanks, I don't want any palaver.' Typical of the humility shown by most of those young men, some of whom were away from home for six years. So, his new medal was put away in a drawer with the rest of his medals. Duty done. A 'no need to keep going on about it' attitude.

We went to the museum's 1940s garden party, and it was very enjoyable. I had only ever been to one such event before. I had suffered one or two health issues and had not been out for some time. My daughter, Trisha, and her husband, Chris, invited us down to their home in a village in Hampshire to give us a break for a few days. On the Saturday they took us for a day out to a local preservation society's forties wartime event being held at Alton railway station, which is also home to the Watercress Line - about ten miles long complete with a steam engine and half a dozen carriages.

People were dressed for the period with British and American military uniforms and forties civilian dress. The men wore trilby hats, wide lapel suits, baggy trousers and braces. The women were resplendent in floral dresses, hats (many with scarf turbans) and we even encountered a group of transvestites enjoying a trip out, dressed in beautifully tailored ladies' costumes, two with neat little titfers on their heads.

There was a 105mm Howitzer outside the station, old military vehicles with trailers, tracked troop carriers which were crawling with dozens of children, anxiously watched by their parents. A half dozen 'Willy's jeeps' with large white stars on their bonnets, a couple of them parked side-by-side with gum-chewing and cigar-smoking guys dressed as G.Is and enough military hardware, it seemed, to equip a regiment.

Children enjoyed organised bike races and a large stage was filled with young men and women jiving and jitterbugging to a big band performing Glenn Miller music. The ladies' skirts flared as they were twirled, twisted and whirled around by their partners to the swing music, defining a generation.

The highlight of the day was the steam train arriving at the station with soldiers and passengers embarking for the ten mile trip along the restored line. Tickets were bought at the ticket office with old shillings and pence purchased before the trip. The station platform was packed with visitors carrying packed lunches. Men and women dressed in British and American uniforms, the men shouldering their rifles and packs all crowded onto the train. The train pulled out of the station amid clouds of steam with soldiers hanging out of the window waving and shouting goodbye. I think, though, the atmosphere was far removed from the troop trains pulling out of stations in the forties…

I don't think I have ever been to an event where everyone wholeheartedly threw themselves into the occasion (I know, I should get out more). Even the weather played its part and it was fine all day. It was truly a very special day for me and one I will always remember.

When I got home, I tried to put down onto paper everything I had seen that day. I have it hanging in our living room now. Not the most brilliant painting, I know, but I never tire of looking at it each and every day as I remember every part of it.

My special day.

A Moment in Time.

CHAPTER 55

Holidays

Life's Little Ups and Downs

We have had some very pleasurable holidays and some wonderful times away with my mother-in-law, Dora. She was pretty long-suffering, putting up with all our trials and tribulations, usually illness with the kids or herself or the car playing up. Dora was, of course, like most nanas - a brilliant childminder - for whom it was a joy to do, not a chore, as she doted on her grandchildren.

We've also had some very happy holidays with my sister, Cynthia and her husband Fred. We once booked a cottage in Tal-y-bont, Wales. We arrived there, for once, without incident. It was a nice cottage, although the kitchen furniture looked like pews that had been rescued from a chapel.

As soon as we got there my husband, Michael, asked Cynthia if he could take Suzy, their spaniel, on a walk down on the beach (like a child, he can't wait to get to the beach.)

'Of course, don't be too long, though, we're getting a meal ready as soon as we've got sorted out,' she said, as he disappeared, leaving us all to unpack the cars and get everything straight.

Off he went to the beach. Suzy thought it was great - she was a little wary of the waves breaking on the beach running towards her and refused to get her feet wet. She went racing away into the distance and Michael could see her little legs waving in the air as she had a good roll in the distant dunes. 'Well, this is a success,' he thought, 'she really loves her first seaside holiday.' However, as he got closer to her, a terrible smell began to hit him. He was horrified to discover that Suzy was rolling in the remains of a dead seal that was decomposing very nicely and she just didn't want to leave it. He finally got her away and took the reeking dog down to the water's edge and tried to get her to go in to wash off the disgusting smell and rotting remains. She was having none of it and in the end, he had to bring her back.

Neither Michael or Suzy were popular for the rest of the day, no matter how much he protested that it wasn't his fault. The appalling smell lingered in the cottage for some considerable time even after she had had a good wash down in the yard outside. No-one really fancied dinner after that.

Our daughter later in the week decided she wanted to go pony trekking. 'No way,' Michael said. 'I'm not letting her go off on her own into the mountains (gentle hills) with people I don't know. I'm going with her.' They asked him if he'd ridden before. 'Oh, yes, loads of times,' he replied (Mablethorpe beach on the donkeys as a kid.) Unfortunately, all they had for him was a very large horse that he swore later he'd seen pulling the milk cart around the village. He said the ride was a nightmare and that he'd never had his legs open so wide in his life. His skinny backside was slipping and sliding this way and that on the very large saddle needed for the horse. He said he felt real despair when they had a little gallop!

He came home walking very peculiarly and when we inspected the damage, his poor backside and between his thighs were raw. I've always regretted not asking my sister to pop her head round the door and take a photo of him

lying there, face down on the bed being tended to, trousers around his ankles with a dressing on each cheek, held on with two strips of micropore tape that looked like two big kisses. I didn't dare though - he wasn't a happy bunny at all and said later it ruined his holiday.

All in all, it was a great holiday, one I fondly remember, and I enjoy looking at those happy people who look so young in the photographs.

Another memorable, if somewhat different, holiday we had was when Michael was injured at work, and he had an opportunity to go to a convalescent home by the sea and I was allowed to go with him. It was a nice place, pleasant bedrooms, excellent, homely food, and spotlessly clean. He had, though, as part of the convalescence deal, got to see the in-house doctor two or three times during the fortnight we were there. I was told I had to go along with him to see the doctor as well. I refused, as there was nothing wrong with me. It was the rules though so in the end, to keep the peace, I went along with him. If the doctor had started snapping rubber gloves on though I'd have been off, quick sharp! Michael was only asked a few questions, and I only had a 'How are you, my dear' from a very old doctor.

Strangely we were told we had to be in by ten o'clock as the doors were locked. Of course, we were late back on our first night. We stood outside at about eleven o'clock like two teenagers, wondering what to do. Personally, I'd have slept in the car rather than cause a fuss but Michael was having none of that, and he hammered on the front door.

It seemed ages before we heard someone coming. I half expected my late dad to be standing there with his hands on his hips saying, 'Where the hell have you been 'til this time?'

The warden opened the door and never said a word. He reeked of disapproval though. We walked into the lounge and all the other residents were sitting there waiting for the next number of bingo to be called by the warden. There were one or two sniggers but bingo soon resumed and our lateness was not mentioned.

They were all very nice people we met at the home. The residents were all injured or ex-miners along with their wives and, as you might expect when such men get together, 'a lot of coal was turned', as the old saying goes, when they started chatting and telling tales of their experiences.

The staff went above and beyond expectations to make everyone's stay enjoyable.

Another nice memory.

CHAPTER 56

A Letter from the Past

The picture in chapter two is of my uncles, Bill and Ted Osborne, Mama's sons and Mam's brothers returning home after the war. I was, of course, too young to remember them going off to the war. Many of our soldiers had been away for years. The picture I painted is a vivid one, in my memory, of them returning home, even though I was so young. It was not surprising really, given all the excitement there was in the house, hearing that they had all survived and were coming home. There was much cleaning and polishing, food to be prepared and their rooms to be readied for when they got back. I have used my painting again as it is relevant to my story.

The excitement of both brothers surviving and being on their way home was unbelievable. The agony and worry that mothers, wives and loved ones went through must have been awful. I had slept with my Mama from birth and did so until she died when I was a teenager. She talked of them constantly, usually when we were tucked up in bed at night, telling me of the escapades they got up to growing up, and the scrapes they had all got into. The picture I painted is of my Uncle Bill, nicknamed by his brothers as Boss (being the eldest) and his brother, Ted. They had returned home and were celebrating after being away for some years. Both had sent strict instructions to Mam and Mama before they got back that they were not to follow the practice that was usual for families of soldiers returning home at that time, which was to decorate the outside of the house with flags and posters welcoming them back.

They had dragged Mama's old and treasured gramophone into the kitchen from the front room and were singing along to old records. I especially remember them singing Jerusalem very loudly, along with the great Caruso, a famous opera singer of that era. They were both well oiled, but they both had lovely, clear tenor voices as young men, and we were all enthralled, apart from our grumpy dad, who they were keeping up with their celebrating, when he had to be up early for work at the Cossall Pit the next morning.

I also mentioned in my previous article that I had received a letter from Uncle Ted whilst he was fighting in the desert in North Africa just before a big battle. That was my first ever letter from anyone and it was treasured. Mama would read it to me every night in bed; it was read so often that it's a wonder we didn't read the words off the page. I have kept that treasured letter all my life and was upset when it went missing a few years ago. It has since turned up again and is now kept safe! It was between the pages of a book I liked. I was lucky to find it.

I thought some readers might be interested in the kind of thing a young soldier then would write to a youngster back home. Here is the letter.

Dear Betty and Baby,

I was very pleased to receive your ever welcome letter saying that you both were well again, also many thanks for the Xmas card and I also hope you had a nice birthday. I'm sorry that I couldn't send you a present but after the war I will take you to the "Three Horseshoes" and we will get drunk on lemonade and ice cream, won't that be nice? I will also buy baby a real live rabbit and you a bicycle. Yes, it would be nice to be home for Xmas, and I would like some Xmas pudding, still I bet I get some corned beef and a piece of heavy duff. Tell your Mam that I want no flags, you can't eat them, but a big fire, a good dinner and a cowboy book.

Well Betty me and my mate have a nice home, it is a tent dug in the ground, as it is warmer like that and much healthier. I have made a stove out of a box, and we have some coal and also a lamp and there are bags of straw, so we are quite well off. I am roasting some spuds at present as we have no chestnuts. Well, sweetheart, I reckon I've told you all the news so I will close, hoping to see you all soon.

With lots of love xxxxxxx Uncle Ted xxxx

PS I hope Santa Clause brings you a lot of things.

Uncle Ted did tell us once how the troops made cookers in the desert to heat food up and to have a brew up. Their home-made cookers he said were far more reliable and widely used, especially by tank crews than anything supplied by the army. I had, however, forgotten how Ted said they used to make them. My husband enlightened me (after he had Googled it!) They were called 'Benghazi Boilers' – petrol and water were transported to the troops in four-gallon tin containers. The tins were pretty thin and easily cut or crushed, not much thicker than today's beer cans and not a patch on the German, so-called, Jerry cans. Those sturdy metal containers were used to transport fuel around for their army.

British troops would cut one of their thin water containers in half, half fill it with sand, punch a few holes in it, then soak the sand in petrol and set it alight. A container of water placed on top of this was brought to the boil very quickly. There were thousands of these empty containers around, so the troops had no problem knocking up a new cooker whenever one was needed.

Shortly after my letter arrived, a battle was fought with the German army. I'm not positive but I presume it would have been fought at El Alamein. Uncle Ted was wounded and sent to a field hospital. He probably thought he was lucky as thousands of young men were killed. Uncle Ted always had a tale to tell. He was a master storyteller and raconteur, but never told us war stories about bullets and bombs. Horror stories were something else though, and he would terrify me to such an extent I would refuse to go to bed alone. Strangely, my Mama, who was usually very protective towards me, with my being nervy, found this amusing!

Until she would say 'Enough, now our Ted.'

My sister never got her live rabbit, and I never got a bicycle, but that didn't matter. Eventually all three brothers were back home, and they spoiled us rotten. I did however get plenty of ice cream and lemonade on the back yard of the Spring Cottage with Uncle Ted. More than once a friend of his would say to him, mistaking me for his daughter. 'She looks like you Ted.' Ted would find this hilarious and say, 'Oh, no, no, that will never happen!' How wrong he was, He was soon married to Freda, and he was gone from our house on Blake Street, soon followed by his brothers. The house felt very empty without their laughing, shouting and fooling about. We all missed them a great deal, especially me, and of course Mama, who would have been greatly relieved at having less washing, ironing and cooking to do, of course, which the woman of the house was expected to do.

Ted and Freda eventually opened a hardware store on Cotmanhay Road, opposite Milton Avenue. Uncle Ted was well known in Ilkeston by just about everyone in the Cotmanhay area, where he would deliver paraffin and sell just about anything you needed from his shop. Ted and Freda had three children, two boys and a girl. When Ted's daughter Janet got married at Cotmanhay church, our daughter was one of her bridesmaids. Most of their generation are now gone. Ted died in 2001, the last to go of the four siblings. My three uncles, Bill, Ted and Ken Osborne, all larger-than-life characters, were lovely, generous men. I loved them all deeply as a child and admired them always.

They are all still missed.

Ted Osbourne, 1942

CHAPTER 57

Men In Sheds

I have, unfortunately, had a number of strokes and the after effects of my illness meant that our already modest social life was brought down to zero. Michael, who had, to put it bluntly, been waited on hand and foot on the home front from birth could barely boil an egg, let alone change a nappy or do any kind of housework.

His idea of having dinner prepared for me when I returned home late from school would consist of a few spuds, peeled and sitting in a pan of cold water waiting for me. He was, to be fair, a man of his time. He worked very hard and often spent too many hours at work. I think it was generally expected and accepted, then, that mothers and wives did all that kind of work.

However, he stepped up to the plate when the chips were down, and I was taken ill. With the help of his mum, Dora, and my dad's sister, my Aunt Barbara, they kept us fed until he had learned basic cooking skills. He did all the housework and whatever needed doing, without complaint. I am proud of him and could not possibly have managed without him.

Because my speech had been very badly affected by my stroke only my immediate family were dropping in to see us. People can find it embarrassing. My best friend and colleague from school came to see me when I got home from hospital. She brought me some carrot cake (although I can't remember much about the visit) and she never came back. I think she was shocked by her changed friend. All these years later she still sends us a Christmas card every year, sending her love and best wishes. Very strange how differently people react to illness.

I wasn't bothered by any of this though. I was happy in my new world with no worries. All of life's worries had been wiped away. I had woken up with a practically blank canvas. I found amusement at the slightest thing, found a love of chocolate and TV cartoons. Where all this came from, I do not know. I couldn't write my name or even do the simplest of drawings for some years. Everything had gone and I wasn't bothered in the slightest. After a few years I became aware that all the time caring for me, after a lifetime of working with people, was not good for Michael but I couldn't do anything about it. So, when he saw an advert in Ilkeston Life, our community newspaper, for a 'Men In Sheds' project for retired men that we had seen being discussed on national TV and that was now coming to a local venue in Ilkeston. He said, 'I might go to that. I wouldn't be gone long - two or three hours a week at the most - you wouldn't miss me.' I gladly encouraged him to go.

So off he went, saying in his own words, 'I'll teach them all I know' (well that didn't take long!) He came home after several sessions and began enthusiastically planning his new project, wanting to test his newfound skills. I watched apprehensively as anything he usually made finished up very big and heavy. 'I'm just off to get some materials,' he said. I thought he was off to Wilkos. I should have known better. He came back from the local woods with all he needed and refurbished all the garden tools, even the line props, proudly finishing them professionally with stain and varnish. Our son scoffed at them and called him 'tight', but to be fair they have all done good service.

The other side of the coin are our very professionally made drive gates, a garden bench with an inscription along the back made from an old bench, refurbished (all completed at Men in Sheds) and one or two electrical jobs done around the house.

He didn't need to admit to me, though, that his supervisory skills were of more use in these projects than his DIY skills. Wonky wall plugs and door handles in our house tell their own tales and are his trademark.

He made some nice friends, who I eventually met and felt very comfortable with. We have all been out for lunch several times and it was so nice seeing them all laughing and joking and to listen to all the banter flying back and forth across the table.

Thank you, Men in Sheds, you have made life a little easier.